Restorative Justice

A GUIDE TO

Making It Happen

Kimmett Edgar is Head of Research at the Prison Reform Trust. He conducted an evaluation of Restorative Justice approaches for the Youth Justice Board as a Senior Research Officer at the Oxford Centre for Criminological Research and also promoted Restorative Justice at the United Nations Commission for Criminal Justice and Crime Prevention. He is the author of *Prison Violence* (Willan Publishing, 2003) – a book that pioneered a conflict-centred analysis of fights and assaults in prisons – and of the Home Office Research Study, *Perceptions of Race and Conflict: Perspectives of Minority Ethnic Prisoners and of Prison Officers* (with Carol Martin) (2004).

Tim Newell is well-known in prison circles and beyond as a former Governor of Her Majesty's Prison Grendon and Spring Hill, from where he took the lead in developing Restorative Justice in three prisons in the first substantial HM Prison Service pilot project during the early 2000s. He is the author of *Forgiving Justice: A Quaker Vision for Criminal Justice* (Quaker Home Service, 2000) and *Murderers and Life Imprisonment* (with Eric Cullen) (Waterside Press, 1999) and was, for many years, the editor of *Prison Service Journal*.

Erwin James was born in Somerset in 1957. A family lifestyle described as 'brutal and rootless' by a prison psychologist following the death of his mother when James was seven, led to a limited formal education. He gained his first criminal conviction aged ten and was taken into care in Yorkshire aged 11. His teenage and early adult years were spent drifting, living with extended family members, and often sleeping rough. He worked in various labouring jobs, but also committed relatively petty, mostly acquisitive, but occasionally violent crimes (criminal damage, common assault). His directionless way of life continued, including several years in the French Foreign Legion, until 1984 when he was jailed for life. In prison he took a degree course with the Open University majoring in History and graduated in 1994. His first article for a national newspaper, *The Independent*, appeared in 1994. He won first prize in the annual Koestler Awards for prose in 1995. His first article in *The Guardian* appeared in 1998 and he began writing a regular column, entitled 'A Life Inside', in that newspaper in 2000. A collection of his columns, *A Life Inside, A Prisoner's Notebook*, was published in 2003. A follow up, *The Home Stretch, From Prison to Parole*, was published in 2005. James was released from prison in August 2004 after having served 20 years to the day, and continues to write for *The Guardian*.

Restorative Justice in Prisons
A Guide to Making It Happen

First published 2006 by

WATERSIDE PRESS

Domum Road
Winchester SO23 9NN
Telephone 01962 855567 UK Low-rate landline calls 0845 2300 733
Fax 01962 855567 UK Low-rate landline fax 0845 2300 733
E-mail enquiries@watersidepress.co.uk
Web-site www.watersidepress.co.uk

ISBN 1 904 380 25 5

Cataloguing-in-Publication Data A catalogue record for this book can be obtained from the British Library.

Printing and binding Antony Rowe Ltd, Chippenham and Eastbourne.

Cover design © Waterside Press.

Internet materials A range of toolkits and checklists in support of *Restorative Justice in Prisons: A Guide to Making It Happen* is available in PDF format at the Waterside Press web-site.

North American distributors /Sole agents:
International Specialised Book Services (ISBS)
920 NE 58th Ave, Suite 300, Portland, Oregon, 97213-3786, USA
Tel 1 800 944 6190
Fax 1 503 280 8832
E-mail orders@isbs.com
Web-site www.isbs.com

Restorative Justice
IN PRISONS
A GUIDE TO
Making It Happen

Kimmett Edgar

and

Tim Newell

With a **Foreword** by

Erwin James

WATERSIDE PRESS

A range of toolkits and checklists in support of this work are available at
www.watersidepress.co.uk

Acknowledgements

We are indebted to many people for their contributions to our thinking. They include many who remain nameless because they are, or were, in custody. We are very grateful to Marian Liebmann, for her encouragement throughout the project and for editing an earlier draft (although, of course, responsibility for any errors remains ours). We have been inspired by the work of the Restorative Justice Consortium, in particular Debra Clothier and Lyndsey Sharpe. Geoff Emerson, David Faulkner, Marian Partington, Charles Pollard, Stephen Pryor, Barb Toews, Barbara Tudor and SACRO also provided helpful ideas. Kimmett would also like to thank Juliet Lyon, Director of the Prison Reform Trust, as well as his colleagues for their support in the work.

Our final words of thanks go to our patient friends, Ann Newell and Madeline Church, who have taught us much about handling conflict constructively and without whom this book would never have been possible.

Kimmett Edgar
Tim Newell

Foreword Erwin James

Crime inspires powerful emotions. How we respond to it as a society causes no end of discussion and argument. Should we punish? Should we attempt to reform? While the debate rumbles on our criminal justice system becomes ever more unwieldy and, as the consistently high re-offending figures show, ever more ineffective. In my view the system's failings are mainly the result of years of disingenuous political interference and negative media portrayal of criminal justice issues, both of which have undermined any chance of real progress being made in this crucially important area of our lives. This may well be the reason why, despite the proven failure of the punitive approach, our society persists in expecting people who break the law to be punished first and foremost with any idea of genuine rehabilitation for the offender only grudgingly and sparingly acknowledged. At the same time the system's consideration for victims of crime, particularly when court procedures are over, is negligible. I believe that given the facts most reasonable people would prefer a better system, one that produced fewer instances of re-offending and therefore fewer victims—a system that could be seen to be working in the very best interests of our society, that we could be proud to own, instead of one that is a source of constant frustration, dissatisfaction, disillusionment and, all too often, shame.

Before going to prison for life I had little idea of what might be expected of me by the prison authorities. I knew that the process I'd been through, the trial and the sentencing, had been fair and just. But as I left the courthouse to be driven to prison to begin my sentence I knew nothing of what lay ahead. Like most people, I imagine, I thought of prison as a punishment for serious wrongdoing. I hadn't considered whether people were sent to prison *for* punishment or *as* punishment—or for that matter, 'rehabilitation.' I had no thoughts about how prison might 'work.' My understanding only went as far as accepting that prison was an inevitable part of my punishment. My learning curve was to be steep.

On arrival the reception procedure immediately made me feel defensive. As a 'new reception' I was locked in a tiny cubicle to await my turn to be 'processed'. Each time a prisoner was let out of his cubicle the rest of us could hear the two prison officers on duty addressing the individual concerned. Invariably the tone was loud and intimidating, 'Right. Stand in front of that counter. Strip. Put your clothes in that box.' Occasionally the officers raised their voices and spoke aggressively to the prisoner. Sometimes they made jokes and laughed. Sometimes they swore. Our civilian clothes, suits, jackets, slacks, designer jeans and shirts, were exchanged for ill-fitting and well-worn underwear, blue striped shirts, denim jeans, and scuffed, down-at-heel shoes. Once dressed, our scruffy, down-beat appearance was in sharp contrast to the smart black and white uniforms of the prison officers, leaving us in no doubt as to our status. This message was further emphasised when it was time for us to be escorted to our cells and we were referred to as 'bodies'. The processing seemed to me to be the beginning of our dehumanisation and its overall effect was that it placed prisoners on one side of the fence and the prison authorities on the other, firmly establishing from the outset the 'them and us' relationship that would from then on exist between us. Significantly, this relationship felt as if it was meant to represent the relationship between prisoners and the society we had been isolated from. Yet I soon learned that there was no sense of common purpose among prisoners. As my sentence unfolded and I moved from prison to prison I learned more and more about life on the inside. On the wings and landings we existed in a state of constant anticipation of the unknown. We distrusted the authorities but distrusted each other more. Sometimes alliances were formed, usually for reasons of safety, and sometimes genuine friendships. But in the main we tolerated each other at best and learned to cope with the enmity, fear and paranoia that the conditions in which we lived generated.

I served all of my time in state prisons. Though I did see physical improvements (after eight years of using a bucket in my cell for a toilet, toilet bowls and wash-basins were fitted in cells in selected prisons throughout the country; in my fifteenth year the authorities began installing electric power points in cells and issuing portable televisions), I saw no change in the system's general attitude towards prisoners. The only element of prison life that managed to counter the powerful sense of social detachment that it engendered amongst us was the input and influence of various individual members of staff who saw their role as enablers rather than punishers. Such people were not confined to any particular department, though the majority whom I encountered were education staff. As the years passed it became clearer that the factor that had the biggest impact on what a prison sentence achieved was the quality of interaction between staff members and prisoners. Staff, who in the course of their work expressed a respectful and helpful attitude towards prisoners, treating us as people rather than just 'cons', had the most influence on the level of personal growth and positive change that any of us might achieve.

In my case I encountered a wing psychologist early on who guided me towards education and — in spite of the fact that I was serving a life sentence and had entered prison with only a limited formal education, huge social failings and no real work skills—worked hard to persuade me that I might still be valuable. (This was in the days before the role of the prison psychologist had been reduced to a mere assessor of risk.) I met others of a similar disposition – the wing probation officer who shared his love of classical music and fishing with anyone on the landing who cared to engage in interesting conversation; the chaplain in a maximum security prison who broke down barriers by casting staff and prisoners in musicals he staged in his chapel to raise money for charity; the cookery teacher whose reputation as a calming influence prompted governors, in awe of her mysterious powers, to send some of their most 'difficult' prisoners to her classes when all else failed. (If they'd sat in once in a while and witnessed the effect that a little trust and common courtesy can have on troubled minds the mystery would have been solved.)

Civilian staff were generally less judgemental and less susceptible to the cynicism of prison culture and therefore easier to engage in honest interaction. But there were uniformed staff too who refused to give in to the destructive powers of prison. An officer came to my cell one day and offered me a job in the Braille transcription unit he ran with a colleague. It was the first time in my life I had ever done anything that might be described as community work. Equally important was that the officer and his colleague made the 20 of us employed in the Braille Unit feel like a much-valued workforce. Later I met staff who taught prisoners to be mentors to groups of people with learning difficulties from local daycentres and special schools. We were buried in the system yet with the help of the kind of people I mention here we were still able and, more importantly, motivated to try to make a contribution to society. Without them it would have been difficult if not impossible to sustain any view of prison as a positive and worthwhile experience. The knowledge that they often had to overcome a lack of resources, overbearing security, and resentment from less well-disposed colleagues in order to bring hope into those places acted as another great motivating factor for many prisoners I knew who became more determined to prove they were worth the efforts made on their behalf.

Nobody I knew in prison expected being in prison to be easy. But neither could anyone understand why prison life had to be so confusing, so chaotic, and so stressful. Or why for that matter the criminal justice system was so divisive. The pockets of humanity that I mention above are proof that, if society chooses, there is another way to respond to people who offend, a way that offers real hope of changing lives for the better. This book provides a framework for a formalised system based on similar principles.

Restorative justice, as the term suggests, involves a process of restoration. The aim is to repair the harm that crime causes, both for the victim and for the offender. Whereas conventional criminal justice strives to be dispassionate and impersonal in its dealings with offenders and victims, restorative justice specifically personalises the process, primarily recognising the equal humanity of both parties. While conventional criminal justice is vengeful and geared to inflicting punishment, that is, inflicting harm on the offender, restorative justice focuses on creating conditions in which a process of healing can take place. It will take courage and commitment from those in positions of influence for it to work in any significant way. But the potential rewards for our society in the long run are immense. At present anyone who offends and succeeds in leading a crime free life after serving their penalty does so in spite of the system and not because of it.

This book shows us that there is another way.

Erwin James
2006

Restorative Justice in Prisons
A Guide to Making it Happen

CHAPTER 1

Introduction and Background

DEFINING RESTORATIVE JUSTICE

Restorative justice is a distinctive philosophy of justice, with a focus on making amends for the harm done. It is also a collection of diverse practices. The theory goes beyond ideas about criminal justice to encompass civil renewal, individual responsibility, conflict resolution, empowerment, shaming and forgiveness. Restorative justice practices have been expanding over the past three decades, as a range of approaches have been applied to different types of problems, including: family relationships; school bullying; training programmes; industrial relations and complaints against the police; in addition to all types of crime. Family group conferences, victim-offender mediation, sentencing circles, peer mediation, circles of support and accountability, and youth panels are methods that have all grown out of restorative justice.

The fundamental principle that sets the philosophy apart is that, when one person has harmed another, the most useful response is to try to repair the harm done. Martin Wright stated this central precept in these terms:

> Restorative justice in the area of criminal justice is based on the idea that the response to crime should be to put right the harm, as far as possible, and not, as hitherto, to inflict harm on the offender. (Wright, 1999: 173)

When a crime is committed, some of the problems that result are addressed by the criminal justice system; other needs are met by restorative justice. The scope of criminal law is limited, in that it deals with people as citizens, as victims or offenders. It is the role of criminal justice to respond to the law-breaking. Criminal justice might address the legal needs of a person who has been victimised, but it cannot solve all the problems that arise for them or the community. For example, it is not the role of criminal justice to provide medical treatment when someone is assaulted. People are far more complex than the roles of citizen, victim or offender. They have many needs that are not addressed by criminal justice. In a 1995 report, the Ministry of Justice in New Zealand cited the role of restorative justice in responding to the emotional dimensions of crime:

> The criminal justice system seeks to deal with crime dispassionately ... Restorative justice recognises the emotional effect of crime on victims, offenders and the community ... Restorative justice seeks healing of the emotional effects of crime as an important part of putting right the wrong. (New Zealand Ministry of Justice, 1995: 21)

People also have moral duties to others that are not laid down by law. Regardless of how far criminal law reaches, there is still a vast amount of behaviour that is not regulated by law. Restorative justice has developed as a method of responding to certain kinds of problems that crime leaves in its wake, for victims, for offenders, and for their communities.

Dan van Ness offered a definition that encompasses abstract principles, good practice and desired outcomes:

> Restorative justice is ... different from conventional justice processes in that it views crime primarily as injury (rather than primarily as lawbreaking), and the purpose of justice as healing (rather than punishment alone). It emphasises accountability of offenders to make amends for their actions, and focuses on providing assistance and services to the victims. Its objective is the successful reintegration of both victim and offender as productive members of safe communities. (van Ness, 1997: 2)

There is widespread consensus that harms to a victim of crime should be made good as far as possible. But restorative justice poses a deeper challenge to conventional criminal justice. As is clear from Dan van Ness' description, restorative philosophy holds that justice requires healing, accountability of offenders and assistance to victims. The criminal justice system is not nearly as supportive of victims, often leaving them with a sense that they have been accessories to a process managed by insensitive professionals.

The primary goal of restorative justice is healing the harms that arise from a crime. In this regard, it is like reparation. Reparation is what the offender gives back to the victim as compensation for the loss of damage caused. A restorative process typically builds a consensus about what harm was done and how those harms might be made good.

However, in most jurisdictions, the scheme for applying reparation is managed by legal authorities. Enforced reparation, imposed by the state or other authority, may address some of the harms caused by the crime, but it ignores the importance of voluntary participation or the choice to make amends by an offender. It also tells the victims what they can expect to receive, rather than listening to what victims feel they need.

Thus while reparation typically encompasses restorative justice aims, like making amends, there is a risk that these processes will fail to meet the individual needs of victims or offenders, precisely because they are imposed by a state authority.

Paul McCold highlighted contrasts between restorative justice and reparation imposed by the state:

> Reparation decided by a judge or a community panel actually interferes with healing as it deprives primary stakeholders of the opportunity to express their feelings, tell their story and collectively identify and address harms, needs, and responses.
>
> (McCold, 2004: 169)

In restorative approaches, the power to decide how to respond to a crime rests with the people who have been most directly affected: the victim, the offender and their supporters.

Central to restorative processes is the right of the victim to put across, in their own terms, how the offence has affected them; how they felt, as the victim. The process respects the wholeness of the person in the way it determines the harm. The harm does not need to be limited to financial terms in order to facilitate compensation. The victim might define how the offence has harmed them by expressing a lasting sense of fear; or self-disgust or increased social isolation.

It is also vital that the offender take responsibility for the final agreement, which would normally include some opportunity for the offender to make amends. In restorative justice, healing actions are voluntarily undertaken by the offender — they are not imposed by the state. Howard Zehr wrote that the offender must be willingly involved in order for the process to be restorative:

> We can require offenders to make right, but they cannot be fully responsible without some degree of voluntarism. (Zehr, 1990/1995: 198)

VARIETIES OF RESTORATIVE PRACTICES

Despite lively debates about restorative philosophy, consensus has been growing about how to define its practices. Tony Marshall's description is widely accepted and quoted. He defined restorative justice as:

> a process whereby parties with a stake in a specific offence collectively resolve how to deal with the aftermath of the offence and its implications for the future.
>
> (Marshall, 1999: 5)

Thus in addition to its attention to harm, another distinguishing trait of restorative justice is that deciding how to respond to a crime is up to the people most directly affected: the victim, the offender, and their circles of support.

Throughout the book, we will refer to the main practices that reflect restorative justice, particularly mediation and conferences. The descriptions that follow are paraphrased from two sources: the websites of the Restorative Justice Consortium (www.restorativejustice.org.uk), and Restorative Justice Online (www.restorativejustice.org).

Victim-offender mediation

Mediation is a process of raising and resolving conflicts by dialogue facilitated by an impartial mediator. In the field of restorative justice and criminal justice, however, mediation usually refers specifically to victim-offender mediation or VOM. The process involves preparation, which allows the victim and the offender to clarify how mediation works, what they want to happen during the meeting and any rules or conditions under which they decide to work. At the meeting itself, under the guidance of the facilitator, the victim and the offender have the opportunity to express their perceptions of the events and the feelings it caused. Victims are able to seek answers to questions that are often neglected by the traditional criminal justice system processes. If a face-to-face meeting is not possible (or not desired) the facilitator can convey messages and questions between the two parties. Victim-offender mediation often concludes with an agreement about what the offender will do to make amends.

Restorative conferences

Conferencing shares some of the characteristics of victim-offender mediation, in that it is a chance for victims and offenders to express their feelings, for victims to make clear what needs have arisen as a result of the offence, and for the offender to clarify what he or she is prepared to do to make up for the harm caused. Conferences differ from mediation, in that both victims and offenders are encouraged to invite to the conference people whom they would turn to for support. A conference decides on the next steps after an offence, by a process of consultation with anyone who has been affected by the crime. Other people can be invited, such as probation or police officers, to represent the interests of the wider community. The supporters – who could be parents, other relatives, friends, schoolteachers, or others – have a role of providing moral support to the person who asked them to attend. Therefore, these participants are sometimes referred to as 'communities of care'. Both the victim and the offender should be able to call on their own community of care to support them through the process. Some conferences follow a script, structuring the process and providing the questions to be asked, in the prescribed order. Others are less tightly structured. But all conferences are meant to work towards a consensus about how to repair the harm done.

Circles and sentencing panels

There is a range of other options which have roots in restorative justice. Among them are circles, in which members of a community are brought together with a facilitator to discuss a problem and work out, together, how the community would prefer to resolve it. A sentencing panel is more often closely linked to the criminal justice system, in that the panel is empowered to decide – often with input from an offender and victim – on a sentence to be imposed, which addresses the harm done and enables the offender to take responsibility.

EMPOWERMENT AND PARTICULARITY

Restorative justice values empowerment, promoting the active involvement of the people most directly involved in a crime. Victims in particular may feel that an offence has robbed them of their sense of control over their own lives. When criminal justice organizes the response to the offence – so that police build up the evidence, solicitors argue for and against the guilt of the accused, and the judge decides on both the finding of guilt and the severity of the punishment – when the criminal justice system monopolises the process in these ways, it reinforces the victims' sense that they have lost control of events.

This is a part of the 'secondary victimisation' which many victims of crime experience in their contact with the criminal justice system. The extent to which legal counsel takes control of the problem is only one way the victim's life is controlled by the criminal justice process. The dis-empowerment of victims is a theme of Nils Christie's argument in his article, 'Crime as Conflict' (1977).

Legal counsel (or, for that matter, the police, judges and other officials working in the criminal justice system) tends to deny victims and offenders a say in what happens in their lives following an offence. Restorative processes are designed to restore to victims and offenders real power to take decisions about the next steps that will dramatically affect their lives. This is perhaps the main reason why restorative processes often operate outside of the legal institutions, and why mediation and conferencing may exclude legal advocates from the list of supporters for either side.

There is another feature of restorative justice that helps to distinguish it from criminal justice. Criminal justice is based on the principle that similar cases should be treated the same. Equal treatment and proportionality mean that the individual needs of people are neglected. Restorative justice focuses on the unique aspects of each situation. Howard Zehr called this value 'particularity' (2003). From the perspective of the people directly involved, their needs are respected and their individuality is valued.

> This value of interconnectedness must be balanced by an appreciation for particularity. Although we are connected, we are not the same. Particularity appreciates diversity. It respects the individuality and worth of each person. It takes seriously specific contexts and situations. Justice must acknowledge both our interconnections and our individuality ... Context, culture and personality are all important. (Zehr, 2003: 35)

After observing conferences in a police-led cautioning scheme in the Thames Valley, Carolyn Hoyle, Richard Young and Rod Hill saw that restorative methods of responding to crime could lead to radically different results in apparently similar cases.

> In a sense, each [conference] was unique in that the circumstances of offences, and the expectations and experiences of offenders, victims and their respective supporters, were diverse. (Hoyle *et al.*, 2002: 6)

This is not an accident, or a trivial characteristic of this experiment with restorative justice. Built into the philosophy and practice of restorative justice is a principle that no two situations of harm arising between human beings are identical. In direct contrast to criminal law, in which the interests of impartial justice are served by treating like cases alike, restorative justice works with people in all their individuality and wholeness. No restorative conference will ever have exactly the same outcome as any other conference, because conferences (unlike courtrooms) honour the individuality and uniqueness of each participant.

There is good moral support for equal treatment as a principle of justice, but it is becoming obvious that the humanity of a prisoner can be lost when he or she is treated just like everyone else. When the treatment that is offered is ideal for a majority, but tends to exclude or disadvantage people in the minority, then proportionality actively works against justice.

As Martha Minow has asked:

> When does treating people differently emphasize their differences and stigmatize or hinder them on that basis? And when does treating people the same become insensitive to their differences and likely to stigmatize them on *that* basis?
>
> (Minow, 1990: 20)

The New Zealand report also recognised this aspect of restorative justice:

> Programme designers cannot know the needs of a particular victim since people's responses to crime are individual. The structure of restorative processes and the focus of any agency administering them would need to emphasise meeting individual needs. Restorative justice recognises that similar criminal offences may have dissimilar effects on victims and offenders, and hence a different or unique response may be necessary to put right the wrong. (New Zealand Ministry of Justice, 1995: 20)

Questions about the meaning of restorative justice have led to detailed statements of basic principles. We refer the reader to three documents in particular: The *Leuven Declaration* (Leuven, 1997); the *Principles of Restorative Processes*, (Restorative Justice Consortium, UK, 2004); and the *Declaration of the UN Meeting of Experts in Ottawa, Canada* (United Nations, 2002).

WHAT IS, AND IS NOT, RESTORATIVE JUSTICE?

Criminal justice agencies, traditionally, have been offender-centred (*Diagram 1*). The central relationship in criminal justice is between the state and the offender.

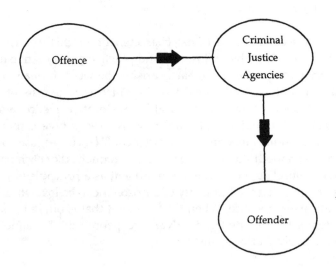

Diagram 1: How the traditional criminal justice system focuses on offenders

All restorative methods reconfigure the relationships that form after an offence. Through restorative justice, it is possible to decipher a conflict underlying many crimes. Restorative justice works with the people mainly affected by the conflict whose views can all be considered in seeking solutions that are just (fair) and can repair the harm. *Diagram 2* shows the more complex setting that restorative justice recognises.

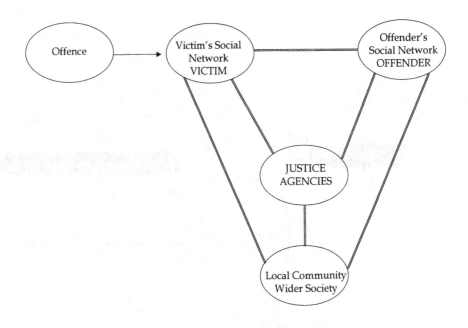

Diagram 2: How restorative justice principles focus on the context and dynamics of conflict

These diagrams, with their contrasting images of relationships, begin to show what is, and what is not, restorative justice.

Paul McCold and Ted Wachtel have proposed that the litmus test of any restorative programme is the extent to which the work involves the three parties who are essential to restorative processes: the victim, the offender and their communities of care. McCold and Wachtel judged programmes to be partly, mostly or fully restorative, depending on how much the victim, offender and supporters were involved. As they stated:

> The degree to which all three are involved in meaningful emotional exchange and decision-making is the degree to which any programme can be termed fully 'restorative'. (McCold and Wachtel, 2002)

A fully restorative process, in their view, completely engages all three parties in the process. And therefore, conferencing is judged fully restorative; a victim-offender mediation is deemed 'mostly restorative' and enforced reparation is seen as 'partly restorative'. *Diagram 3* (designed by McCold and Wachtel) represents their ideas.

The three parties do not only need to be involved, but they need to be central to the process of building a consensus and to have a genuine influence on the agreement. The test requires programmes to work towards specific goals for each of these stakeholders: repairing the harms suffered by the victim; encouraging responsibility in the offender; and finding reconciliation of the problem within the communities of care (families and loved ones of the victim and offender.)

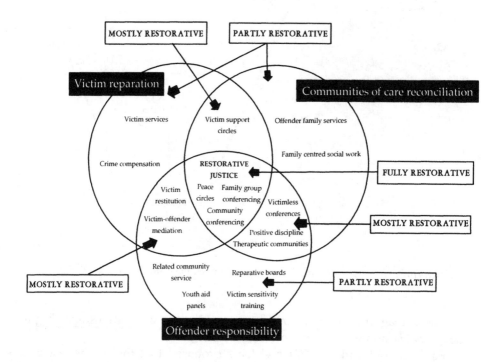

Diagram 3: Based on McCold and Wachtel's diagram of restorative approaches

A scheme that repairs the harm but fails to empower the core persons (victim and offender), as enforced reparation would do, is only partly restorative. A scheme that involves dialogue but does not vindicate the victim (as a no-blame approach might do) is partly, but not fully restorative.

McCold and Wachtel checked the accuracy of their model by measuring the success of conferences, mediation and comparison methods and then comparing their measures to the kinds of restorative practices being used. They found that the programmes they defined as fully restorative (involving real engagement and input from all three stakeholders) were more likely to provide satisfaction to the victims, and to be seen as fair by offenders.

Given the debate over the definition and values of restorative justice, it is extremely helpful to have a tried and tested tool for evaluating practices. However, their scheme is not the only possible way of deciding whether a particular approach is restorative. Their test is tied to a particular restorative method (the conference). Their interpretation of true restorative justice is based on two principles: (1) the process should involve victims, offenders and supporters; and (2) the results should be considered satisfactory by the victim and the process should be seen as fair by the offender. Participation in decision-making, victim satisfaction and offender accountability are not all that restorative approaches can (or perhaps should?) offer.

A different test would begin by assessing how well a programme fulfils other core restorative principles. Dan van Ness defined restorative justice with reference to a continuum on four distinct measures (van Ness, 2004), see *Diagram 4*. Each continuum highlights important characteristics of restorative justice and provides for a method of testing any particular intervention.

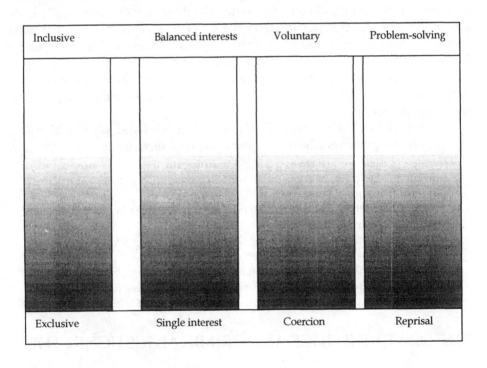

Diagram 4: Van Ness' diagram of the central values of restorative justice

Using this measure, interventions are most restorative when they:

- involve the participation and engagement of victims, offenders, their communities of care and other concerned individuals;
- recognise and work to meet the interests of a wide range of people, and are not targeted at a specific outcome (e.g. reconviction rates);
- build on the basis of informed choice for all participants and do not require any individual to attend; and
- aim for solutions to the problems raised by the offence, and see reprisals as the lowest priority in responding to the harm.

In addition to these tests, a case could be made for restorative justice to be the best means of resolving the conflicts that result from a crime. If we take this view, processes would be judged by how well they resolve conflicts between the main parties. For some types of crimes, the underlying conflict might be resolved more fully if privacy were given a higher priority than being open to wider participation.

In practical terms, dialogue is the first step because it is how the process defines the harm done. The second step is empowerment, as victims, offenders and their supporters decide on what to do. The third step chronologically is the action taken by the offender to repair the harm. The characteristics that make restorative justice unique might be these steps, but in reverse order: repairing harm, empowering victims and offenders, and engaging in dialogue to resolve differences. This list of priorities implies yet another test, judging a restorative justice programme by its success in healing harms, empowering participants and resolving conflicts.

The report by the New Zealand Ministry of Justice listed key characteristics of restorative approaches which incorporate many of these tests:

- a definition of crime as injury to victims and the community peace;
- a focus on putting right the wrong;
- a view that both the victim and the offender are active players in responding to and resolving the criminal conflict;
- empowering victims in their search for closure through direct involvement in the justice process;
- an objective of holding offenders accountable for their actions;
- impressing on offenders the real human impact of their behaviour.

(New Zealand Ministry of Justice, 1995)

RESTORATIVE JUSTICE AND CRIMINAL JUSTICE IN THE UK

What are the purposes of criminal justice? The question drives the political agenda but also raises legitimate issues about justice in a society. The public concerns about what criminal punishment should achieve are:

- it should protect innocent law-abiding citizens from the harms the law is designed to prevent. It should do this by encouraging citizens to obey the law. The aim of law is to maintain a morally acceptable community;
- offenders should receive their just deserts. The moral idea is that the punishment should fit the crime;
- it should redress the injustice done by the criminal offence by requiring offenders to pay for their wrongdoing. The moral concern is that when a wrong is done to someone, justice requires that it be made right. There is also the assumption that the wrongdoer should make it right; and
- punishment should not make the offender worse. Ideally it should make him or her a better person, through moral reform, therapeutic cure or conformity through social integration.

Criminal justice practice reflects at least four distinct philosophies of punishment:

- retribution;
- deterrence;
- rehabilitation; and
- social defence.

Retribution holds that punishment is good as an end in itself because wrongdoing deserves to bring harm upon the wrongdoer. It claims to uphold human dignity by respecting the capacity for free choice between right and wrong. Retribution is perhaps best known as 'an eye for an eye', because it is also based on the principle of proportionality: the punishment should fit the crime.

Deterrence means that the basic function of state punishment should be to prevent crime by threatening people with painful consequences. Deterrence has a number of components, and these must work together to produce any deterrent effect. The person must know in advance about the law and the punishment. The chances of detecting the crime must be good. Having been caught, the person must expect punishment (it must be certain). And the punishment needs to be severe enough that the anticipated pain of punishment outweighs the benefits of committing the crime. If a punishment is not effectively deterring criminal behaviour, this might be because any one of these steps has failed. Yet, too often, a knee-jerk reaction assumes that a harsher punishment will correct the problem.

Rehabilitation emphasises the reform of offenders. The theory is that people commit crimes because of some defect that can be identified, treated and cured. Thus, rehabilitative punishments focus on programmes applied to the offender. Currently, offending behaviour programmes and sex offender treatment are based on rehabilitation. Rehabilitation philosophy can be linked to indeterminate sentencing, so that a prisoner is kept inside until the authorities are persuaded that he or she is sufficiently reformed that the public will remain safe when they are released.

Social defence theory is based on the view that the function of the penal system is to protect society from crime. One way this might be achieved is to incapacitate dangerous people by imprisoning them. While someone who has committed robbery is in prison, they are not committing crimes on people outside. However, social defence is a wide-ranging theory which aims to develop measures based on scientific evidence about what reduces crime.

These perspectives do not always work together harmoniously. Retributive philosophy declares that each person is responsible for the consequences of their actions, whereas rehabilitative theory tends to emphasise the needs of offenders for treatment to help them control their behaviour. Deterrent theory advocates increasing the severity of punishment if crime persists, whereas rehabilitation would argue that more damaging punishments make re-offending more likely. Social defence analysis of a person's risk of re-offending might mean that they remain in prison after their (retributive) sentence has been served.

Table 1 contrasts retributive and rehabilitative responses. Retribution places full blame on the individual who has broken the law, and responds punitively by depriving them both of freedom and responsibility. Rehabilitation also deprives the individual of responsibility, but it does so by defining the offender as someone who was incapable of exercising responsibility.

As for the practice of criminal justice, we believe that it does not fulfil — indeed, it is not designed to fulfil — all of the main purposes that the public, the judiciary and politicians demand from the justice system. The restorative focus on those most directly affected by a crime, and restorative justice's problem-solving and future-oriented methods, make it an ideal complement to the criminal justice system, addressing some typical dilemmas of each theory of criminal justice:

- for retribution (or 'just deserts'), community and victim have a say in what should happen as a result of the crime;
- for deterrence and social defence, offenders report the process as more demanding than the court process but also more respectful;
- for rehabilitation, the community and the victim are involved with the offender often in taking part in a treatment plan.

Restorative approaches provide for wide discretion in tailoring the conflict resolution of all the factors in the crime setting. Restorative justice also provides for restitution, making good the damage brought about by crime. Restorative justice transforms the dichotomies between deterrence and rehabilitation, or between retribution and rehabilitation, while it shares common goals with all of them. Offenders are censured and called to account (retributive), they have issues to work on for the future (rehabilitative) and have an opportunity to make amends to the victims they have harmed (reparative).

	Welfarist Rehabilitation	Correctional Treatment	Restorative Practice
Causes of crime	Primarily structural, social and economic	Primarily individual/familial	Breakdown in relationships; contextual disruption
Responsibility for crime	Primarily the state's	Primarily the offender's	Offenders and their Communities of care as well as paucity of opportunities
Characterisation of criminal	Unfortunate individual for whom assistance is required	One of a deficient and/or dangerous group (classified by risk) from whom society is to be protected	People who have not been aware of their behaviour or the effect of it on others
Characterisation of practice	Offender-oriented assistance and protection from further damage by the system	Public-oriented punishment, management and treatment	Community, victim and offender-centred practice seeking to enable those affected to take responsibility for healing the harm
Characterisation of rehabilitation	Rights-based restoration of citizenship	Utilitarian re-education for citizenship	Putting right what has gone wrong; restoring relationships
Practice focus	Diversion from custody, practical help, advocacy, seeking opportunities	Enforcing punishment, managing risk, developing skills through (enforced) treatment	Facilitating dialogue between stakeholders to empower them to take responsibility for putting things right
Intended outcomes	Re-integration of the offender	Punishment of the offender and protection of the public	Repairing the harm for the victim, the community and the offender

Table 1: *Contrast of three paradigms for work with offenders*

RESTORATIVE JUSTICE AND PRISONS

Some commentators see restorative justice as completely opposed to retributive justice (the term used by Howard Zehr (1990/1995) to refer to the guiding principles for the way criminal justice has been practised by the police, the courts and prisons). Others see the two as complementary. We fall somewhere in between. Although there are ways that retributive practices and restorative justice can complement each other, the profound differences between the two need to be acknowledged and respected.

Our basic purpose in writing this book is to contribute to the growth of restorative processes in prison. We believe that restorative justice has great potential to humanise prisons, improve safety, enhance social order, and make the experience less hostile and damaging for all concerned. We believe that a completely transformed prison, centred on restorative values, would:

- begin to address society's obligations to victims of crime;
- serve as a place of safety in mediating between people who have been deeply harmed and those who have caused the harm; and
- occupy a crucial position in the reintegration of offenders into society.

The main obstacle to this goal of the restorative prison is a deep tension that needs to be acknowledged from the start. On one hand, there is the view that restorative justice is a soft option. From this perspective, prisons are meant to be punitive, and any notion of making them less damaging would detract from their roles of retribution and deterrence. On the other hand, there are restorative justice advocates (and others) who believe that imprisonment is so damaging that the only way forward is to abolish prisons. From the first perspective, introducing restorative justice into prisons is viewed with suspicion, as a way of making custody too easy for criminals. From the second perspective, restorative justice totally contradicts the use of punishment and prisons.

Russ Immarigeon described the distance between restorative justice and prisons in these terms:

> Incarceration is the institutional manifestation of the punitive impulse that restorative justice is designed and intended to challenge. (Immarigeon, 2004: 150)

If he is right, then the whole point of prisons is to punish; the whole point of restorative justice is to heal; and the two cannot be reconciled. From this perspective, there is only one criterion by which restorative projects should be judged: their effectiveness at steering offenders away from the inevitably damaging experience of prison. Restorative projects must, by this test, be diversions from custody.

When restorative justice and prisons are defined as opposites, every move by a prison system to treat prisoners with greater respect can be viewed with suspicion. Immarigeon quoted two apologists for restorative justice who feared that prisons would exploit the reputation restorative justice has built up.

We must avoid the danger that imprisonment, with all its known disadvantages, is 'packaged as restorative justice.' The hijacking of restorative justice initiatives is a real threat, certainly when it concerns a possible new legitimation of imprisonment.

(cited in Immarigeon, 2004: 143)

If restorative justice can be linked to prisons, this might make imprisonment more attractive to the courts, and, through 'net-widening' increase the problems of overcrowding. For example, if courts decide to use restorative justice agreements as conditions for community sentences, and sanction any breaches with prison, then restorative justice processes could result in more people being sent to prison.

The fact that we are writing this book shows that we do not accept the terms of this interpretation: we do not see restorative justice and prisons as opposites by definition. Nonetheless, we respect the tension between the two. In one sense, our answer to the tension is a consistent thread throughout the remainder of this book.

Carolyn Boyes-Wilson described the distance between restorative philosophy and the criminal justice system in stark terms:

The state operates through impersonal and rationalized procedures administered by disinterested professionals with specialized legal, administrative and penal expertise. The goal is to punish, manage or rehabilitate people who violate the law in order to maintain control over its jurisdiction. Restorative justice, by contrast, seeks to delegate decision making and control to those individuals directly involved in the incident. The goal is to harness the power of relationships to heal that which has been harmed and to empower the community to engage in processes of repair, reconciliation and redemption in order to restore balance in the wake of harm. (Boyes-Wilson, 2004: 215)

But unlike restorative theorists who argue that restorative justice should pursue a totally separate path, Boyes-Wilson embraced the creative tension between the two:

The incompatibility between the institutions of the justice system and restorative justice may generate a kind of creative tension that opens space for the transformation of those institutions. (Boyes-Wilson, 2004: 216)

In a similar vein, Barb Toews works promoting restorative philosophy to prisoners near Philadelphia. She defends her work in prisons by raising tough questions about the impact of restorative justice on prisons, and the effects of prisons on restorative justice. With Jackie Katounis, she wrote:

We are challenged to explore what restorative justice, as a philosophy, has to say about the prison environment itself …

Is restorative justice possible in prison without challenging the violent and punitive prison values and practices?

Without challenging the prison environment, are we condoning violence and saying that harming offenders is OK?

… Is restorative justice about transforming people's lives to the fullest extent possible or only to the degree we allow while punishing them?

Can restorative justice resist co-optation by the values and practices of prison?

Does punishment and prison even have a role in restorative justice?

(Toews and Katounis, 2004: 112-113)

Here are some of the main limitations of the prison that we believe impede its capacity for restorative work:

- *coercion* – running an institution by giving orders and backing them up with punitive sanctions limits empowerment;
- *separation* – a structure designed to maintain physical separation between the victim and the perpetrator cannot facilitate dialogue to the same degree as a more open setting;
- *controlled regime* – these limit the offender's opportunities to make amends. An offender in prison could not offer to compensate the victim directly by, for example, painting his or her fence or digging the garden; and
- *punishment* – the punishment at the heart of imprisonment is the deprivation of liberty. Thus every encounter between a victim and his or her offender would take place in a setting that fundamentally restricted the options available to the offender.

Recently in England and Wales, restorative approaches as a diversion procedure for young and minor offenders have expanded. The public perception of restorative justice is possibly only a partial image, due to the publicity given to work with youth. But when restorative justice is thought to be limited to its practice with young offenders in the community, the wider relevance of the philosophy can be neglected.

While restorative justice and prisons continue to be seen as opposite points of the spectrum, the potential of restorative justice to work with serious offending will be severely restricted. The victims of serious crimes are let down when prisons are not used as places of restoration for offenders, victims and their communities. Prisons are full of people in desperate need of restoration – those most damaged and damaging in our society. Unresolved conflicts about their relationships with their victims and their community often remain within the person no matter how many personal development opportunities for change and learning they have taken in prison.

So, how can a prison provide restorative opportunities? Marian Liebmann and Stephanie Braithwaite produced a summary of restorative work being undertaken in prisons in 1999. We refer the reader to that work, acknowledging that in this field things change very quickly. We will not attempt to provide an up-to-date report on all the restorative work in prisons at present. Rather, we can take a broader view by listing some of the developments that show how restorative justice can be used to good effect within prisons. Some of this is based on the restorative justice in prisons project that Tim championed just before leaving HM Prison Service.

To set the scene for the areas we discuss in this book, some of the obvious areas for restorative approaches in prison are:

- meeting the needs of crime victims, including (but not limited to) developing victim empathy in prisoners, facilitating victim-offender mediation or conferences and prison outreach to victims' groups;
- making amends — opportunities that enable the offender to repay the victim (e.g., via a trained probation officer's facilitation); also indirect reparation (for example, through Inside Out Trust workshops or through charity jog-a-thons);
- offender restoration and rehabilitation, by taking full advantage of offending behaviour courses, and/or drug and alcohol treatment;
- staff industrial relations, including the provision of mediation for disputes arising between members of staff; and
- operational functions, such as discipline, complaints, sentence planning, maintaining family ties, and pre-release work.

The capacity of a prison to benefit from restorative justice depends primarily on making the environment safe. Unless prisoners can be free of victimisation while they are in prison, they are unlikely to be able to focus their attention on those they have damaged by their offending behaviour. Thus the need to create and sustain safe, healthy prisons is vital for the future development of restorative justice in prisons. Restorative practice can help this process through a change in the typical methods of managing conflicts inside — and this is why there is such potential for restorative justice to influence operational functions in prisons. We have made the point that restorative justice restores relationships and brings a problem-solving focus to incidents of harm.

An underlying theme throughout this book is the impact of restorative justice on the traditional responses to trouble. The questions at the heart of the restorative justice response are simple, but when asked in settings that are safe and respectful, they can lead to remarkable results:

- Describe in your own words what happened.
- What were you thinking at the time?
- Who do you think has been affected by what happened?
- In what ways were they affected?
- What should happen to put things right?

Consider how these questions could influence the ways officers conduct induction, sentence planning, or in dealing with disputes between prisoners. Consider how senior management could use these questions in facilitating adjudications (disciplinary hearings), responding to prisoner complaints or dealing with officers' concerns.

CONCLUSION

The potential for restorative justice in prisons is considerable. It should not be seen primarily as a tool towards reducing recidivism (although there is evidence that this will happen) but as a means towards empowering offenders to take responsibility for their actions and to make amends to their victims and their communities. Nor should the work be entered into without much preparation and careful development, based on experience. The Prison Service[1] lacks experience in restorative justice work and should consult with practitioners in the community where there is established expertise.

To build a consensus that prisons can become more restorative cannot be done without this partnership. To sustain this work in prisons the offering of support must come from the community. Guided by restorative justice, prisons can become true places of healing and transformation for the community as well as for those directly affected by crime: victims and offenders.

In the chapters that follow we will first discuss the fundamental values of restorative justice (*Chapter 2*). In *Chapter 3*, we set out a model of organizational culture and change. *Chapter 4* brings to light conventional views in HM Prison Service, to suggest how these assumptions might lead to obstacles for the further growth of restorative justice approaches. In *Chapter 5*, we explore programmes and functions a restorative justice prison would produce. *Chapter 6* explains the concept of a responsible sentence, and the implications of the Social Exclusion Unit's report on re-offending by ex-prisoners. *Chapter 7* concludes with a guide for criminal justice practitioners.

---

[1] All references to 'Prison Service' are to HM Prison Service/UK prisons unless stated otherwise.

CHAPTER 2

Restorative Values

THE CORE VALUES OF RESTORATIVE JUSTICE

- Healing
- Voluntary participation
- Respect
- Empowerment
- Inclusiveness
- Equal status
- Personal accountability
- Problem-solving

The first step in promoting the use of restorative justice in prisons is to deepen understanding of the core restorative values — what really matters in the philosophy. In *Chapter 1* we discussed two tests for restorative justice projects. McCold and Wachtel advocated a test based on the extent to which victims, offenders and their communities of care were engaged in the process. Van Ness suggested four continuums to emphasise restorative justice's principles of inclusiveness, balancing interests, voluntarism, and problem-solving. Debates within the restorative tradition focus on a recurring list of values. We examine these in more detail here.

Healing
Healing the harm is the essential aim of restorative justice. Any crime has multiple effects. The criminal justice system focuses on crime as an attack on the authority of law. Criminal justice processes are designed to reassert the legitimate authority of the law. But a crime always has other consequences. Most acts deemed criminal result in harms to someone (or to a group of persons).

The harm done varies enormously, depending on the nature of the crime and the circumstances (and perceptions) of the victims. Restorative justice processes must be, first, about identifying and clarifying the harm done (beginning with the victim's experience) and second, about a collaborative method to find possible solutions to the problems caused by the crime. If a response to crime is not based on finding ways of healing the harms caused by the crime, then that response is not restorative justice.

Voluntary participation
The principles of restorative justice spell out the need for the voluntary participation of all the parties. For example, the United Nations' Meeting of Experts in Ottawa, Canada, stated the principle of voluntarism in these terms:

Restorative processes should be used only where there is sufficient evidence to charge the offender and with the free and voluntary consent of the victim and the offender. The victim and the offender should be able to withdraw such consent at any time during the process. Agreements should be arrived at voluntarily and contain only reasonable and proportionate obligations. (UN 2002: 4, para.7)

Free and voluntary consent to the process and outcomes is, like most values, difficult to define and measure accurately. What does it mean to participate voluntarily when you are in a prison? Real choices are made in the midst of many factors that might influence one's choices, including the extent to which one's peers knew of the situation and made suggestions; attitudes reflecting the person's home life or neighbourhood values that guided them in making their choice; and many other motives that are personal. Is it voluntary if a prisoner says she wants to take part because her boyfriend suggested she should?

The value of voluntarism means that participants need to decide for themselves to take part. A key aspect of the decision to take part is *informed* choice: potential participants must have the opportunity to have restorative processes explained fully to them before making a decision to take part. Indeed, there is increasing support for the principle that victims should be given a choice which restorative approach they would prefer to use.

Paul McCold has made the point that retributive justice does things *to* offenders; rehabilitative work does things *for* offenders; and restorative justice works by doing things *with* offenders. This introduces a central difference between restorative justice and established prison practices. It is also a very helpful test of prison programmes: if they are not based on working *with* offenders, if they are doing things for or to them, then there is a good chance that the programme is not restorative.

Voluntarism is equally important throughout the process. While it is a valid part of conferences for facilitators to put questions to both parties, neither should be compelled (or feel under a compulsion) to disclose more than they want to.

A different interpretation of voluntarism holds that victim participation should be entirely voluntary, but offenders should participate because the harm they have done has placed an obligation on them to make amends. It is also possible that an offender who denies responsibility in court may be more willing to address the harm they have caused if they are in direct contact with their victim. Over time, the extent to which participation is voluntary can change.

Respect is a wide-ranging value that encompasses all aspects of the ways victims and prisoners are treated. At a basic level, it is an unconditional obligation. As a former Chief Inspector of Prisons, Sir David (now Lord) Ramsbotham wrote:

In committing offences prisoners have often shown little respect towards others, but the negative behaviour demonstrated through crime can never be used as the reason for not giving prisoners the respect that is due to them as human beings.

(HMCIP, 1999: 60)

Many current procedures in the criminal justice system fail to meet this standard in the ways they treat people suspected (or convicted) of offences.

In prisons, officers and other staff—including healthcare personnel, teaching staff, and others—also deserve to be treated with respect. This means, at a minimum, that they should be consulted in developing restorative programmes within the prison.

Respect is a quality of relationships that must be maintained throughout restorative processes. At the same time, conferences and mediation are intended to allow victims and offenders to be open about their feelings. It is challenging and essential to balance the principle of maintaining respectful behaviour with being open to the expression of genuine feelings.

In the aftermath of a crime, when one of the parties has been defined as the perpetrator, or the criminal, it can be extremely difficult to respect the offender as a human being. In restorative justice processes, respect is put into effect by:

- listening to everyone's input, and not interrupting;
- taking into account their views when making decisions;
- speaking politely; and
- ensuring that each person is able to maintain their dignity.

In any conflict situation, part of the problem is that different interpretations of the same events can be seen as contradictory. In a search for hard facts, two opposing views might emerge and there may be a temptation to judge that one or the other point of view is deceitful. Respect is a power that enables the participants to value their diversity, and see that both perspectives might be valid.

Helen Bowen, Jim Boyack and Chris Marshall wrote:

All human beings have inherent and equal worth irrespective of their actions, good or bad, or of their race, culture, gender, sexual orientation, age, beliefs or status in society. All therefore deserve to be spoken to and treated with respect in restorative justice settings. Mutual respect engenders trust and good faith between the participants. (Boyack, Bowen, and Marshall, 2004: 270)

Empowerment

The aftermath of a crime requires decisions about what should be done next. Empowerment emphasises that the problem behaviour and how to respond to it are owned by the people most directly involved (see further, Nils Christie, 1977). Authority to define actions and decide on future solutions rests with the person who was harmed, the person who committed the harm, and their communities of support.

Tony Marshall's definition (1999: 5) of the restorative process helpfully shows that responsibility for finding solutions lies squarely inside the conference or mediation. Deciding on how to meet the harms should be up to 'those with a stake in the outcome', that is, the people directly involved in the situation and their respective networks of support.

Restorative outcomes work best when the response has been determined by the participants; they work least well when participants have had 'solutions' imposed upon them by authorities who have been unable to surrender their power to distribute blame and to decide on a fair outcome. Charles Barton showed the importance of empowerment in ensuring that the processes being evaluated are genuinely restorative:

> Restorative justice fails in cases where one or more of the primary stakeholders is silenced, marginalised and disempowered in processes that are intended to be restorative. Conversely, restorative justice succeeds in cases where the primary stakeholders can speak their minds without intimidation or fear, and are empowered to take an active role in negotiating a resolution that is acceptable and right for them.
> (Barton, 2001: 70)

Empowerment is a deeply challenging principle, but without it, the power of restorative justice to engage all parties to the offence is weakened, and the criminal justice system will continue to fail to meet the needs of victims of crime.

Inclusiveness

The inclusive approach of restorative justice means that each participant has a chance to speak freely and have input into the decisions. The knowledge that one will have an opportunity to speak provides a sense of security in the process. It is closely linked to the value of empowerment, because through inclusiveness, the participants are reassured that they will have a say in the task of dealing with the harm.

> Restorative justice processes require more than the presence of the offender: they require their inclusion. They are expected to directly participate in the process, to speak about their offending and matters associated with it, to interact with the victim ... and to contribute to decisions about the eventual outcome. From all this offenders are expected to have a better understanding of their offending and its consequences, to become accountable for the offending in ways which they understand.
> (Morris and Young, 2000: 17-18)

Inclusiveness highlights a desire to find processes in which victims and offenders (and their supporters) can feel involved and can gradually achieve a sense of working together towards common goals. There are two obvious points at which this value distinguishes restorative justice from current criminal justice practice.

Restorative processes—mediation, conferences or circles—work with conflicting perspectives to lead participants towards a consensus, a sense of teamwork in solving the problems generated by the crime. In contrast, the criminal court pits representatives of the state against the offender in a battle to win the case.

Further, while the ultimate 'solution' in criminal justice is banishment in prison, the vision of restorative justice is to create peace in the community. This recognises that banishing people does little to resolve the issues and creates serious problems of social exclusion (see *Chapter 6*). Offenders are part of the community and their resettlement is eased if the relationships they have with their communities of support and care are nurtured. Cavanagh commented:

> The community of the offender includes family, friends, and work relationships. Those relationships provide the environment for developing a sense of social

conscience, awareness of how one's actions affect other people, and a desire to be a positive member of the community. (Cavanagh, 1998)

Equal status

Equal status is complicated, particularly when a typical conference identifies one party as the victim and the other as the perpetrator, even before the conference begins. In broad terms, however, it means that restorative processes maintain the dignity of both parties.

The theory of 're-integrative shaming' which is considered by one school of restorative philosophy to be central to the process of the conference, carries a particular understanding of guilt, which is non-stigmatising. John Braithwaite argues that the traditional courtroom process has four attributes that confirm the offender in his criminal role. First, the procedure is humiliating. Second, the passing of sentence defines the offender as a deviant, but there is no parallel ceremony to mark the re-integration of the person as a full citizen. Third, the court condemns the offender as an evil person. And fourth, Braithwaite argues, the criminal behaviour is allowed to become an enduring part of his or her identity (1993: 37).

Observations of conferences led Braithwaite to see that the process requires the offender to face up to the harm he or she has done in a way that reinforces his or her citizenship status and sense of belonging in the community. Re-integrative shaming describes a psychological process by which the offender comes to share the community's disapproval of his or her harmful actions. An essential factor in this model is that the offender is joined in the conference by people who mean the most to them — their 'community of care'.

Braithwaite believes that four aspects of a restorative conference are vital to make the re-integration work: First, the process balances disapproval with sustained respect for the person. Second, there is a way to mark the behaviour as deviant, but there is also a rite to signify that the person is welcomed back into the community. Third, the disapproval is targeted on the deed, not the person. And therefore, fourth, the person does not incorporate deviance into his self-image.

The presence of the community of care is important. They can offer the offender moral support through a difficult process. But equally, their reactions to hearing what he or she has done can awaken feelings of empathy in the offender.

Restorative justice distinguishes between actions and persons, condemning the harmful act whilst providing support and respect for the person who caused the harm. This distinction enables the process to work with both parties on an equal basis, and to recognise that both the victimised and the victimiser have a story that deserves to be heard and considered in decisions about next steps.

The explicit guarantee of equal status means that restorative structures provide enormous security for the personal integrity of all participants. That is, the process will not be one in which they are talked down to, or in which actions are taken, decisions made, without their input. Restorative facilitation requires an ability to serve the conference or mediation by taking a back seat and encouraging the participants to negotiate and develop solutions.

Equality also refers to the purposes of any restorative approach: a conference, mediation or circle is not convened to meet the needs of the offender, nor are these methods victim-centred. If either emphasis becomes disproportionate, then the imbalance detracts from the impartial, healing focus. This is how we interpret van Ness' point that restorative approaches are not single interest.

Victims have a variety of needs, as do offenders. The differences in what they want to achieve require sensitive facilitation to achieve a fair outcome. To complicate matters, it cannot be assumed that the aims of both parties will be self-serving, that victims will want compensation and offenders will seek forgiveness. When a victim wants to use the conference to ensure that the offender gets the support they need to turn away from crime, and when the offender wants to use the conference to work out how to reassure a victim about the risk of future crimes, then the offender's goals are victim-centred and the victim's, offender-centred.

Personal accountability

The judicial trial defines the offender's action as an offence against an abstract legal code; not, primarily, a way that the offender has hurt another person. In practice, holding citizens accountable to the legal code rather than to other people tends to drive them away from victim empathy. Further, in court, the input of the victim is controlled and minimised, so that the offender rarely gets to hear directly from the victim about the experience, in his or her own terms.

In contrast, restorative values hold that each person is accountable to the other stakeholders *as persons*. At a minimum, this sets out a structure for the restorative process in which each person knows that their rights to an equal opportunity to speak and to be heard with respect depend on their willingness to listen with respect to the others. But its deeper meaning is that we are all responsible for how we treat others, whether or not what we do falls within the rules.

In the conference, personal accountability also means that each person knows that he or she will be asked to explain their perspective on events to a meeting gathered to establish the truth of what happened. This aspect of accountability creates a powerful incentive to be truthful. The adversarial atmosphere of the courts aims to ensure truth-telling by the threat of punishment, while the structure provides some incentives to exaggerate. Crime victims who don't have any other way to influence sentencing may tend to suggest that blame lies entirely with the accused, while the accused, fearing punishment, has good reason to deny responsibility.

Equal status and personal accountability work together when the offender is able to feel that, although their behaviour is condemned, they themselves are accepted and respected as fellow human beings. It can be difficult to ensure that the process clearly distinguishes between the person, who is respected, and the act that is condemned. But the gain is that the offender often is able to reject the harm which they committed while seeing themselves as part of the solution.

Restorative processes have been experienced as a tough option. This is partly because they do not excuse the offender, as arguments drawn from deprivation or social exclusion might do. Rather, the process condemns actions while maintaining respect for, and the equality of, the person who caused the harm. The aim, as Gerry Johnstone has written is 'to persuade offenders to share the community's judgement of their behaviour.'

> Those deemed responsible for committing a crime will not be judged as severely as they are in retributive justice. Condemnation of their behaviour as unacceptable to the community will be mixed with empathy for them as members of the community who have erred. At the same time, it will be made clear that the circumstances which might mitigate their guilt do not excuse their actions and, crucially, do not remove their liability to make amends for the harm they have caused. (Johnstone, 2002: 93)

Problem-solving

Problem-solving means processes are restorative when they look forward to ways of healing the harm done. The problem-solving emphasis requires a shift from the assumption that the natural process in criminal justice is to follow a finding of guilt with a punishment. Instead, a restorative process is based on responsibility, not guilt, and on problem-solving, not punishment. (This is not to say that restorative agreements must preclude any punitive element but any punitive outcome must be shown to contribute to solving the problem, or healing the harm.)

PROGRAMME INTEGRITY

Respecting restorative values and keeping alert to the ways prisons can undermine them help to ensure that a project is genuinely restorative. The question of whether a specific initiative is truly restorative is one of programme integrity. We shall turn, later in this book, to some of the particular ways that restorative values are put at risk in prison. But first, we consider how programme integrity has been assessed in work outside prison. Although this revisits the ways that restorative justice is defined, here the main emphasis is a practical concern about how to ensure that what is being done is in line with restorative justice values.

David Miers *et al.* conducted an evaluation of a range of restorative projects. The range of practices was sufficiently broad to question whether some of the schemes qualified as restorative justice:

> Although these often included 'victim awareness' sessions, contact between the scheme and victims, let alone arranging 'mediation', was not a high priority and there are serious doubts as to whether they can reasonably be called restorative justice schemes at all. (Miers *et al.* 2001: 2)

In their evaluation of the Thames Valley work, Hoyle and her colleagues applied a simple test to the conferences they observed. These were scripted conferences, in that the facilitators had been trained to follow a set agenda of clearly defined questions as they ran the conference. Hoyle *et al.* judged the conferences by how well the script was adhered to. They found that the sessions in the early stages departed so profoundly from the model in the script that they could not legitimately be termed restorative:

> Only two of the 23 cases we observed merited the label of restorative justice in that they adhered closely to the Thames Valley model and were therefore restorative in nature. (Hoyle *et al.*, 2002: 13)

Problems of programme integrity have also surfaced in meta-analyses: evaluations that combine a large number of separate projects. The Canadian Ministry of Justice Research Division used the following definition as the basis on which to include data on the outcomes of restorative programmes:

> Restorative justice is a voluntary, community-based response to criminal behaviour that attempts to bring together the victim, the offender, and the community in an effort to address the harm caused by the criminal behaviour.
>
> (Department of Justice, Canada, 2001: 5)

This definition is quite broad, yet consider the hidden biases it contains: It omits reference to the reintegration of victims and offenders, limits restorative justice to matters of criminal law, and fails to give priority to the central aim of healing rather than retribution. Equally, by stressing its voluntary character, and placing it in the community, this definition would rule out schemes run by government, or those that operate inside prison.

PRESSURE POINTS IN THE DEFINITION

The Canadian definition is cited to illustrate the key dilemma in evaluating restorative projects. Restorative theory is clear: translating it into practice inevitably generates tensions between the aspirations of restorative justice theory and the challenges arising from practice. Such pressure points raise a number of questions about the criteria of programme integrity in evaluating initiatives that claim the label 'restorative'. For example:

- Are programmes legitimately restorative if control is maintained by the criminal justice system?
- Is direct contact between the victim and offender a necessary condition of true restorative justice?
- Are there practices or outcomes, such as a strong element of punishment that, if included, mean that the initiative is not restorative?

The literature underlines the importance of values such as empowerment, voluntarism, equal status, and non-punitiveness. We suggest that any restorative practice will find conflicts between the core values of restorative justice and the apparent demands of practice.

For example, a current evaluation is basing its approach on a random selection. The researchers hold the view that a random sample is necessary to demonstrate conclusively whether restorative justice can prevent re-offending or not. But immediately a tension arises: if the offenders who take part in the conferences are selected at random from those who are willing, then the values of voluntarism and empowerment suffer.

What are the pressure points for restorative justice in prison? The central purpose of the process is to bring healing. Despite the benefits that victims can gain from meeting the offender, many victims of crime may also find prisons an intimidating environment. An emotionally vulnerable victim may find comfort in the restorative intervention while simultaneously experiencing some emotional trauma from their brief experience of prison: the banging of gates, the frisking by an officer, a sense that they are treated in an impersonal manner by staff, or even indignation at the disrespect a particular officer might show to the offender.

Prisons tend to be hierarchical, punitive and dis-empowering: therefore we might usefully think about how restorative justice in prisons might come up against pressure on its commitments to equality, to healing and to enabling offenders to take responsibility for their actions.

Two pressure points for the restorative justice value of empowerment concern process and outcomes. The first is the likelihood that prisoners and prison staff will be unfamiliar with the process of a restorative conference and will therefore need a strong model of the method before they can use it well themselves.

The second is the risk that prisoners or staff might bring punitive values to the conference, using their turn to speak to stigmatise the other party, or insisting on severely punitive agreements. In practice, the aspiration of empowerment may encounter a pressure point in the terms of agreements generated by the parties. For example, an agreement, with the free consent of the offender, might require longer incapacitation in prison.

Prisons are coercive institutions, and therefore any voluntary programme raises questions about whether the prisoners are genuinely free to decide not to take part. A pressure point on voluntarism is the degree to which the restorative aims are influenced by the alternative of a punitive response. For example, if mediation were used to deal with a complaint against an officer, and if she believed that if she did not take part she risked being dismissed, would her participation in the mediation be voluntary? Yet, the goal of eliminating all punitive elements from responses to harmful behaviour is possibly unworkable in a prison.

John Braithwaite and Heather Strang recognised the tense relationship between conferences and punitive aims:

> While it is important that threats of escalated enforcement action never be made in a restorative process, it is pointless and counterproductive to deny them as a possibility. Any criminal justice encounter involves an implied threat of coercion … It is best they be kept in the background rather than the foreground of deliberation; but if they are not there at all, we are not dealing with a criminal justice matter, nor with a criminal law enforcement process that is likely to afford prudent protection to citizens. (Braithwaite and Strang, 2001: 211)

Another pressure point in practising true voluntarism is the person's lack of familiarity with the concept and practices of restorative justice. The evaluation of the Thames Valley conferences linked voluntary choice to preparation beforehand, to give would-be participants sufficient information about the options: 'If participants do not know what to expect from a restorative cautioning session then what have they consented to?' (Hoyle *et al.* 2002: 19).

This principle makes clear that restorative justice works best when the participants understand, in advance, what the process entails and decide on that basis that a conference or mediation is the method they choose to deal with the problem. However, a degree of encouragement might be beneficial in persuading someone to try an approach that is unfamiliar to them. But threats of an adjudication (for example) exemplify the kind of coercion that inevitably compromises the restorative spirit of the process.

PARADIGM SHIFT OR EVOLUTION?

In his pioneering work, *Changing Lenses* (1990/1995), Howard Zehr drew on the philosophy of science to suggest that restorative justice would lead to a paradigm shift in responding to crime. The retributive paradigm of determining guilt, assigning punishment, and harming the harm-doer would be replaced by the restorative paradigm, according to which, doing harm creates the obligation to make amends. The new way of responding to a crime would be to identify the harm done and negotiate how it might be resolved. Criminal (retributive) justice was the punitive way to reaction to a crime; restorative justice was the healing response.

According to Zehr's original argument, retributive and restorative justice were polar opposites. In the hands of the criminal justice system, retributive justice neglected the victim and stole the conflict, taking control over the destiny of the offender. The new, restorative paradigm recognised the needs of victims and would expect offenders to take responsibility for the consequences of their decisions and to make amends for the harm they had done.

The benefit of Zehr's scheme was that it advocated restorative justice as an alternative to retributive justice. When victims felt re-traumatised by their contact with the criminal justice system; when the public saw the costs of prison rising but they felt no safer; when the impact of imprisoning rising numbers of people became more obvious; restorative justice offered a very different way of dealing with crime. Although Zehr has moved away from such a polarised view (2002), there is still evidence that the criminal justice system ignores the needs of victims and insulates offenders, through imprisonment, from the actual harms caused by their actions.

The problem with language about paradigm shifts is that it promotes either/or thinking:

- *either* crime is defined as rule-breaking *or* as harm to people and relationships;

- *either* a criminal can be sent to prison *or* an offender can take part in a restorative conference;
- *either* offenders are diverted out of the criminal justice system through restorative justice *or* restorative justice brings more people into contact with the police, courts, and prisons; and
- *either* society reduces the number of people sent to prison, *or* restorative justice has failed.

The extreme result of describing restorative justice as a paradigm shift is the suggestion that we need to dispense with the criminal justice system entirely, abolish prison, and rely only on mediation, conferences and sentencing circles. This is hardly a reassuring message for judges, the police, Prison Service personnel, or indeed, ordinary members of the community!

A broader view of the developments in criminal justice over the past 20 years shows that restorative justice has had a huge influence on the practice and processes of criminal justice. It is not a case of a once-for-all paradigm shift. Rather, restorative philosophy has been the catalyst for an evolutionary development in the way societies respond to crime.

Here are just a few examples of the changes that chime in with the restorative philosophy:

- victim support;
- family ties in prison;
- the work of the Prisons and Probation Ombudsman;
- the expansion of neighbourhood mediation;
- increased involvement of the voluntary sector in prisons; and
- community liaison groups working with local police forces.

The public does not need research to prove that restorative justice works but it does need greater familiarity with the key concepts of restorative justice and experience of it in action. They need to become familiar with what it stands for, how it works and what it achieves.

At the same time, people who work within the criminal justice system can perform a crucial role in expanding the application of restorative philosophy. The achievements of the Thames Valley Police in pioneering restorative cautioning are a prime example. One of the roles of the police is to maintain social order by demonstrating the power that the state has over its citizens. The Thames Valley Police made a commitment to facilitate restorative justice conferences wherever possible as a first response to youth crime. Their commitment went far to establish restorative cautioning as an official, authoritative method of responding to first offenders.

The essential contribution to restorative justice made by professionals working in the police, the courts and the National Offender Management Service (NOMS) requires them to take on board the core restorative values and processes (such as empowerment and equal status; mediation and circles of support) and find new ways of using these in the functions that they now perform within the criminal justice system.

CHAPTER 3

Organizational Culture

INTRODUCING RESTORATIVE CULTURE INTO PRISONS

This chapter discusses the potential of restorative principles and practices to transform prisons at three levels: projects, establishment (individual prison) and total organizations.

Restorative projects have been shown to bring benefits in:

- meeting the needs of victims;
- helping offenders take responsibility for their actions and reduce their rate of offending; and
- helping communities of care to become part of the process of reconciliation and support.

But what can restorative work offer to influence the way that prisons are managed? How broad can the impact of restorative justice be? How can restorative justice benefit everyone who is affected by what happens in prisons?

Conventional methods of running prisons have evolved as a response to the inherent conflict involved in keeping people in custody against their will. They are also rooted in historic values regarding serious offenders. Criminal justice systems define offenders as those who must lose their freedom so that society can feel safe. Thus, serious punishment and prison become joined concepts in public thinking.

Restorative approaches to crime and conflict resolution represent a cultural challenge to the attitudes and assumptions that dominate prison governance and dynamics. To implement restorative practices in prisons — and, in particular, to use circles and conferencing approaches — calls for an examination of the tensions between the paradigms of current penal practice and restorative justice.

The word paradigm comes from the Greek *paradigma*, meaning pattern or example. The function of the paradigm — on which all organizations and bureaucracies rely — is to define the organization's purpose. An institution's paradigm maintains its identity, reflecting taken-for-granted assumptions, concepts, values, perceptions and shared practices. The paradigm forms a particular vision of reality, the ethos or culture.

The dynamics of bureaucracies are self-preserving and preoccupied with internal processes of enforced compliance and maintenance of control systems. Restorative principles can assist the Prison Service to become more effective in pursuing many of its goals. But the fundamental challenges restorative justice poses to the prison paradigm must be recognised. In the context of overcrowding, restricted resources and performance testing, the current prison paradigm gives staff emotional support, offering stability and a consistent purpose. The contrasting paradigm of restorative justice can inspire a creative problem-solving approach which has much to offer prison staff in this pressured setting. To make the most of the opportunity, the dynamics of culture change need to be explored.

Restorative approaches promote four goals:

- to enable victim, offender and community to work together to understand what happened in the crime/conflict;
- to realise who was affected by the events and how;
- to decide together what should happen in order to repair the harm; and
- to consider what can be arranged to help prevent the repetition of the harm.

By their nature, prisons isolate offenders from their communities and out of contact with their victims. Despite this, prisons present tremendous opportunities to use and to develop restorative principles. Equally, the four goals of restorative processes hold out great promise to address the issues which prisons are most anxious to tackle. Adopting a restorative philosophy can provide the foundation for a culture-changing process for prisons, enabling them to become more effective in meeting the long-term real needs of offenders, victims and their communities. Restorative work can also make prison a more harmonious environment, within the boundary of the institution, for prisoners, their families, staff and management.

In considering the potential for restorative approaches applied in prisons, it is helpful to have a sound model of organizational and cultural change, one that will enable us to see where and how a system can begin to meet needs more effectively. The Prison Service is dissatisfied with certain manifestations of its culture and is working to change them: for example, levels of violence, victimisation and intimidation, serious disruption, and racial discrimination.

ORGANIZATIONAL CULTURE

Our model of cultural change in institutions has been developed with the Management School at Cranfield University. It provides a way of understanding change in complex organizations and systems. Accurately seeing the obstacles that hinder change in the prison as an organization depends on an awareness of the prison's fundamental beliefs and assumptions (its culture). A cultural web can be used to group together the different components of a prison's organizational structure (see below).

The paradigm is a vital feature of organizational life. If managed properly, it encapsulates the distinctive competencies of the organization and the system within which it operates. In addition, it can provide a formula for success that will allow the organization to develop. If mismanaged, however, it will act as a conservative influence to prevent change. Indeed, a stagnant paradigm can cause a drift away from key objectives and lead to poor performance. The paradigm can be managed and transformed by analysing the cultural web that maintains the paradigm. The elements of the prison's culture involve security, punishment, deprivation, separation and survival as well as safety, respect, purposeful activity and resettlement procedures.

Much of the influence of culture is through assumptions and routines that are never made explicit, and rarely talked about, so that bringing them to light can be complicated. The cultural web is comprised of the six dimensions that, together, make up the organizational paradigm.

Observation of an organization's functions gradually reveals its culture. We can draw out clues about taken-for-granted assumptions from such observations, like trying to describe an iceberg by observing the parts of it that show and inferring what the submerged part must look like.

These elements, shown in *Diagram 5*, are interdependent and often very deep-rooted within the life and history of the organization. We will explain the six dimensions of the cultural web and then relate each to the reality of prison experience. In *Diagram 5*, the elements in the darker circles on the left are deeply rooted in the organizational subconscious whilst the other three are more immediate, and thus more readily accessed by management consultants. However, changes within these latter areas may not affect the long-term changes required because they do not reach the full culture of the organization.

Diagram 5: The cultural web

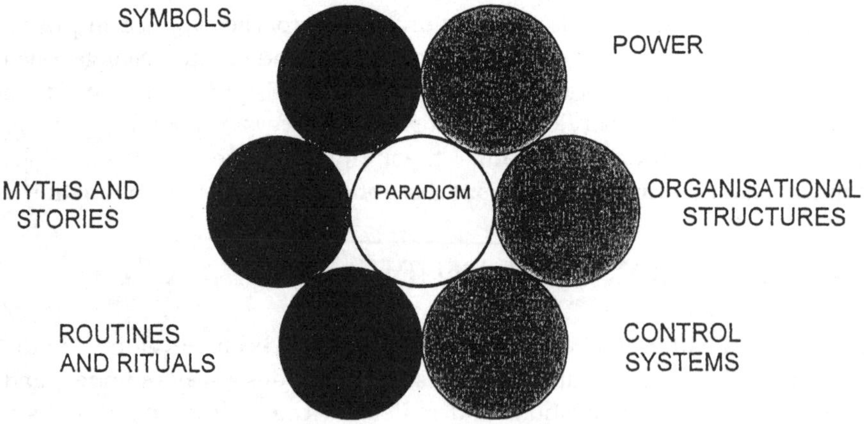

SYMBOLS

POWER

MYTHS AND
STORIES

PARADIGM

ORGANISATIONAL
STRUCTURES

ROUTINES
AND RITUALS

CONTROL
SYSTEMS

THE CULTURAL WEB OF PRISONS

The six dimensions of the cultural web are:

- power structures;
- organizational structures;
- control systems;
- routines and rituals;
- myths and stories; and
- symbols.

Let us look at each of these in turn. We will first describe the conventional prison cultural web, element by element, and then look at how restorative culture could change the prison's web.

Power structures
Power structures or hierarchy reflect the effort and drive required to carry out the essential work of the organization. The explicit structures reflect the formal arrangements as described; but within those structures are the informal power arrangements through representative and networking arrangements. The structures show the formula for success and need not be based upon seniority — technical expertise can be significant as well.

Prison power structures tend to be rigidly hierarchical. The Governor at the top directs the senior management team which in turn organizes prison officers to carry out the work of controlling and caring for prisoners. Each layer of the hierarchical pyramid is directly accountable to the one above: thus, prisoners are answerable to uniformed staff; wing officers are accountable to middle management (including principal officers and senior officers) and middle management is responsible to senior management. When conflicts or crises arise, there is a strong temptation to rely on established procedures. Executive decision making is a preferred method when reacting to immediate and severe problems.

Prisons are places where power is very important in maintaining the balance of co-operation in the dynamic life of the institution. Officers have legal powers to maintain control of prisoners. Staff have legal authority to use force when necessary to maintain the integrity of the prison.

But prisoners have power, too. The concept of legitimacy refers to the conditions that make the prison experience more or less acceptable to prisoners. In most prisons, basic functions like laundry, food preparation, cleaning, painting and decorating, and garden maintenance are carried out by prisoners. If they withhold consent, the prison stops. The powers of prisoners are derived from their numbers, from their compliance and involvement in the regime, and from their hold over sub-cultural activities and relationships.

The strict hierarchy brings with it an ever-present possibility of resistance. Prisoners can rebel against their bottom-rung status by direct or indirect means. But a significant area of power for prisoners is the influence they command over their peers. For many prisoners, the peer pressure they face can have a greater effect on their behaviour than the prison rules or regimes.

Organizational structures

'Organizational structures' refer to the formal arrangements made by the organization to describe its working patterns. These often reflect the power and relationships within the organization. Hierarchical structures reflect the idea that strategic decisions remain the preserve of the top layers whilst everyone else is working to orders. Increasingly however, these are flat structures with layered hierarchies. Effective organizations have open and organic structures, reflecting the rapidly changing emphasis of operations and priorities.

Conventional prison organizational structures are triangular (management, staff and prisoner), hierarchical and divisive. This is because boundaries are essential for roles to be developed through organizations. According to this model, prisoners are at the bottom of the organization, and management directs the staff to manage and control the prisoners.

Control systems

The control systems of organizations monitor the distribution of resources. They often constitute hard plans for the future work, defining priorities and key indicators of performance. They also contain soft systems such as induction programmes for staff joining the organization and the appraisal system that connects individual commitment to the work of the organization. Measurements and rewards emphasise what is important to monitor and recognise.

An example of a control system in the Prison Service is monitoring of performance. Key Performance Indicators (KPIs) and Key Performance Targets (KPTs) are systems of monitoring that enable management to keep an eye on staff. Targets also measure what is done with prisoners: for example, the number of prisoners who have completed an offending behaviour course in a year is recorded and monitored.

Common control systems to manage prisoners are:

- the Incentives and Earned Privileges system, which sanctions prisoners' institutional behaviour by rewarding compliance and reducing regime entitlements/enhancements for prisoners whose behaviour is disruptive;
- the pay scale for prisoners' jobs; and
- the disciplinary system, which aims to reduce harmful conduct through a legalistic and punitive process.

The control systems of prisons have their own logic, based on three steps: the first is to target an individual, the second is to separate them, and the third determines what is done *to* the prisoner.

Richard Sparks and his colleagues have written:

> The primary device for the control of problematic situations in prisons is provided by some form of movement of prisoners within and between institutions, and ... this is principally exclusionary or incapacitative in effect rather than positively oriented towards facilitating improved behaviour. (Sparks, *et al.* 1996: 312)

Let us consider how prisons typically respond to self-harm, drug misuse and risks to personal safety (victimisation).

There are humane and caring ways that prisons address self-harming behaviour. However, the first step, both chronologically and in terms of importance for prison staff, is to register the individual prisoner as someone at risk. Officers do this by filling out a form (the F2052SH) that sets out the evidence for targeting the prisoner. The prison's processes of addressing someone's tendency to injure themselves begins with identifying them as a self-harmer.

Drug misuse is also handled through identification and targeting. Prisons practise Mandatory Drug Testing (MDT), a programme that subjects one in ten prisoners, chosen at random, to a urine test which can determine whether they recently consumed an illicit substance. Prisons assess people's levels of drug dependency and suitability for treatment. The bedrock of the prison's policy of reducing drug misuse is the identification of prisoners who have drug misuse problems.

Prison management makes use of two different tools to enhance the personal safety of prisoners: the disciplinary system and anti-bullying strategies. Both are powerfully determined by the principle that the primary task of officers is to identify individual prisoners who pose a risk to the safety of others. In virtually every prison there is a strict anti-bullying policy, which includes posters warning prisoners not to bully others; an anti-bullying committee (or anti-bullying co-ordinator), and a process which sets out how to find out who are the bullies. Once they are identified, the anti-bullying policy sets out the steps to take.

Equally, control over social order is pursued through disciplinary systems based on requiring officers to identify culprits and provide sufficient evidence against them to convince the Governor that the charge is reliable. (See *Chapter* 5 for a fuller discussion of violence reduction and anti-bullying.)

Banishment, separating certain individuals from society, is the most basic function of prisons. Thus, it should come as no surprise that, faced with a problem, the stock method prisons use to control prisoners is to separate the 'problem individual' from others. Separation is so tightly woven into the way prisons deal with people that most prisons have a distinct area known as the Segregation Unit. The prison is not the only social institution that runs on the principle of separation. In hospitals, the same principle is called quarantine.

Regimentation might enable a prison to get through a day smoothly, but it also means that prisoners are told when to get up and assigned particular times for eating, using the phone, having a visit with their family, or going to education. By its nature, and by necessity, given the pressures of regulating the movements of large numbers of people, the prison works on the basis of doing things *to* prisoners.

Routines and rituals give meaning to everyday activities and define important relationships. They reflect what an organization celebrates and rewards in small but significant ways. Routine ways that members behave toward each other and towards those outside the organization make up 'the way we do things here'. At its best this lubricates the working of the organization. It can also represent a taken-for-grantedness about how things should happen, which is extremely difficult to change.

Rituals are special events through which the organization emphasises what is particularly important. These can be relatively formal processes such as training programmes, interview panels, promotion procedures and conferences. They can also be informal matters like drinks in the pub, or gossip around the photocopier.

Various rites can be distinguished and often feature deeply in people's consciousness. These include rites of:

- passage (induction, training events);
- renewal (project teams);
- integration (Christmas parties);
- conflict reduction (negotiating committees);
- degradation (firing top people, demotions or 'passing over');
- sense-making (rumours, surveys to evaluate new practices);
- challenge (new behaviour of top executive); and
- counter-challenge (grumbling, working to rule).

Prisons are very strong on routines and rituals. 'Regime' from 'regimentation' shows how central routine is to prison life. The need to impose order on possible chaos places a strong imperative on staff to routinise many activities. Making an exception often causes an inconvenience, disrupting the flow of the routine. Hence, the need for organizational efficiency reinforces the value given to conformity to patterns and procedures, despite the cost of denying people their individual voices and personal responsibility.

Regularising activity and behaviour so that most people realise what is expected helps to manage anxiety levels. The daily miracle of the large local prison looking after 1,400 people in a small, confined setting is a case in point. Its ability to provide work, education, exercise and association for most prisoners, with a compliant response, is indeed a miracle. The 'bell' is a celebration in many prisons (marking the start and end of certain activities). Reward is often given to those who can understand and work within the rules — they are selected to be orderlies or given other desirable jobs.

Myths and stories

These are the stories which are shared among members of the organization about themselves as individuals and about the organization as a whole. They are told to each other, outsiders and new recruits. They present the history, the events and the personalities in accessible form. They feature successes, disasters, heroes, villains and mavericks who deviate from the norm. They describe the kernel of truth about the organization; they reflect its dominant values, or ethos.

Each prison has its own traditions. There is often a resistance to learning from the practice of other prisons and from excellence in other settings. It is a matter of emotional involvement and survival as to why each prison develops its culture and its culture carriers. These may often be reinforced by the routines and rituals referred to above. These 'carriers' are often the longest serving and most respected staff — not necessarily the senior ones. It is a real accomplishment if a manager can get into the position of being so respected. Stories often describe critical incidents and how the staff settled them or did not. Attitudes to prisoners and their families are developed through this tradition as well as through experience of success or failure in working together.

Symbols

These are the signs and emblems that the members of the organization recognise as standing for them. They can include the leaders of the organization. Often, the key symbols of an institution refer back to events, actions, or physical features — logos, offices, titles, language, uniforms, standardised design and architecture. How people are referred to (as customers, service users, residents, trainees, or 'screws' and 'cons') plays an important role in influencing the strategy of an organization.

Prisons have many strong symbols: the wall, the gates, the uniform (of both prisoners and staff), the rule book, the hierarchy, the description of being Her Majesty's Prison, the Centre of the prison and so on. The way prisoners are addressed symbolises an attitude that reflects roles and expectations. To use only someone's surname rather than their given name or using Mr or Mrs before the name shows that the person is fundamentally different in their role. The former Director General, Martin Narey, in inviting staff to use the formal titles of address, raised a hornet's nest of complaints that reflected the subconscious role of such symbols in keeping the paradigm safe.

RESTORATIVE INFLUENCES ON THE CULTURAL WEB

Traditionally, strategic change in organizations has focused on the first three elements: power structures, organizational structures, control systems. These tend to be the most recognised and easily influenced areas of work, partly because they are the most tangible.

However, it is often the case that the last three elements — routines and rituals, myths and stories, symbols — may put up the strongest resistance to cultural change. This is particularly so if the reforms challenge the valued 'truths' of the institution's existence. Rituals, myths and stories, and symbols are difficult areas to address as they are rarely talked about in organizational culture. They are taken for granted and are deeply incorporated into members' feelings about belonging.

In order to be effective, strategic change must affect all six elements of the cultural web. Only by working out a strategy that addresses all six can managers and those who seek to reform ensure that the change will have a lasting effect and become fully incorporated into the life of the organization. The cultural web can be used to identify the features of the criminal justice system that must be addressed to bring about change in the direction of restorative values and aims.

The original paradigm of the criminal justice system centred on the need to protect the public by minimising the risks that offenders represented. The means chosen to reduce the risk reflected a philosophy of retribution. Prison, as the most serious penalty for offenders, represents the most psychologically painful expression of our disapproval. It represents (and has done since prison became the substitute for transportation) getting rid of, or making an outcast of, someone. However the myth of 'out of sight' being 'out of mind' can become dysfunctional when those people leaving prison are more damaged as a result of their experience.

As society aims to make prisons more effective in restoring prisoners to community living, there is a need to counter the repressive elements that have formed the paradigm over the years. The change towards a more restorative paradigm or culture can be seen emerging in some aspects of our approach towards community justice. The process through which this is done will afford power to individual prisoners to accept responsibility and to influence the outcome of the process in a more direct way than ever before. There are signs that a major paradigm shift is occurring in addressing social exclusion. Restorative justice has the potential to make an important contribution by transforming the culture within which society responds to offenders and victims.

What do the elements of the cultural web, for example, power structures, symbols and control systems look like from the perspective of restorative philosophy? How might restorative justice re-shape the cultural web we have just discussed?

Power structures
In contrast to the hierarchical shape of power relationships in prisons, restorative processes work by relying on a flat power structure. In a conference or mediation, any power disparities between individual parties should be minimised by the process. One of the inevitable consequences of restorative approaches is that prisoners are empowered, as people whose lives will be affected by decisions about the prison, to exercise their input into how the prison is run.

To see prisoners as partners in the organization of a prison marks a dramatic cultural shift from a more traditional structure in which prisoners are assigned a passive role. Recent years have seen an expansion in the range of opportunities open to prisoners to contribute to the life of the prison community. Examples include:

- education, in which prisoners may volunteer to tutor their peers;
- suicide prevention, through the Listener programme; and
- prisoner councils, responsible for representing the concerns of prisoners to senior management.

Restorative justice implies a profound change in the power structure of the separate sub-cultures in prisons. Restorative justice encourages prisoners to take personal responsibility for their offending and to make reparation to those they have harmed. It counters the culture of secrecy and close camaraderie that normally prevails among prisoners. It implies a degree of overt power-sharing that can be very different from the expectations of many staff. It contradicts the stereotyped perception that prisoners are incapable of exercising personal responsibility in acting accountably. It challenges the assumption that they remain in the role of offender through denial and dependency, that they cannot break free and become responsible citizens. It also challenges the social separation between staff and prisoners, which is often a matter of psychological survival in systems of coercion and overload.

The dynamic of a restorative conference setting or circle in which all participants are able to make a contribution to the resolution of a dispute counters the conventional approach of prisons which develops dependency in prisoners so that they fit into the system of the institution and are easier for staff to regiment. A power structure based on control over prisoners is replaced by working with them to share power over decision-making. As a direct consequence, what the prison provides is far better suited to the actual needs of prisoners.

Organizational structures

We have said that, by convention, prisoners are at the bottom of the organizational structure of prisons. By contrast, restorative justice sees offenders as partners, with a vital stake in the community. Clearly, this represents a tension for many prisons. Despite this, partnership approaches are developing, in suicide prevention work, diversity and equality issues, prison councils (see Prison Reform Trust, 2003) and educational programmes of peer counselling. The prisoner's role as stakeholder is given its fullest expression in therapeutic communities where each person (from management, staff and prisoner groups) is responsible for his or her decisions and accountable to the whole community. In these contexts prisoners are encouraged and trained to take responsibility in exercising leadership within their peer group.

Restorative justice also sees offenders as accountable to their victims outside, with an obligation to put right the damage they have done. In contrast, prisons are defined as the penalty for the crime. Technically, once the sentence is completed, the prisoner has completed his or her obligation to society, and is free to pursue a normal life. Clearly there is tension in this difference between holding the offender accountable to the victim and viewing prison as the punishment.

Restorative justice's flat power structures, open approach to communication, and sharing of issues in direct ways challenge prison expectations about secrecy and management information systems. This is because restorative justice expects people to be willing to give an account with openness and honesty, trusting others to work with the material in responsible and accountable ways.

Control systems

Restorative approaches can work in all systems. If restorative philosophy is accepted fully and across the board, then its principles can affect all involved, staff, users and stakeholders. The use of restorative thinking in everyday life leads us to expect everybody to take responsibility for their actions and be willing to give an account when their behaviour affects others. Under restorative justice, control systems are more consensual, operating with the agreement of all concerned. In the next section, we will follow a disciplinary process to illustrate how this control system might be transformed by restorative justice.

Restorative justice can also be used in induction programmes to engage officers and prisoners in the decision-making process, asking them to use a problem-solving and inclusive approach in their role inside.

In the conventional system, key performance indicators, based on output and outcomes, are used to control activities of management and staff. By contrast, restorative justice is particularly concerned with process and with the values that inform that dynamic. Outcomes remain important of course, but they may take longer to achieve. That is because to pursue outcomes in restorative ways must engage all of the stakeholders or parties in the process of deciding. This tension between process and outcome can be marked at times, but can lead to significantly different feelings of involvement of participants.

Voluntary compliance with agreements is known to attain higher levels of implementation. Restorative processes promote internal controls that can contribute to the institutional reform agenda, which could reduce costs, improve services and deliver a more agreeable workplace.

Routines and rituals

Restorative processes have their own routines and rituals. These are meant to promote the values of empowerment, healing and taking responsibility. Routines within restorative approaches lead people to expect that their worth as individuals will be respected. Everyone has his or her say and only one person speaks at a time (with some token to mark the speaker). The routines celebrate the possibility of transforming harmful conflicts and achieving agreement. Thus it is important to note that restorative justice does not reject routines and rituals. Indeed its effectiveness depends in part on an established set of assumptions and activity.

Myths and stories

Restorative justice will gain the confidence of participants through the successful involvement of people in the process. Although it sounds very rational and common sense, the experience of involvement is not something that can be explained or prepared for. The formative myths of a prison grow out of significant events in the past life of the institution. In exactly the same way, the myths that sustain restorative justice will grow as managers, staff and prisoners gain more experience of it. It will prosper as its myths and stories are told, shared and understood.

Stories and celebrations follow naturally from victims experiencing something that addresses their needs, from prisoners finding understanding and support, and from community members witnessing to the power of the process.

Symbols

Restorative justice also has its symbols. A major symbol is the circle. Others are the agreement, the facilitator (entrusted with the leadership of the process), or the handshake at the end of a conference. In some meetings, a talking stick (a carved stick or eagle's feather) is the symbol of a commitment on the part of all present to practise respectful listening.

Lode Walgrave contrasted the symbols that represent criminal justice against restorative symbols:

> The criminal justice system is captured in the image of Lady Justice balancing her scales. Blindfolded under the pretence of fairness, she is frequently unable to see the experiences of those impacted by crime. Restorative justice removes the blindfold, exposing the people — victims, offenders and community — to full view.
>
> Restorative advocates have created their own images to represent the philosophy. Many use the image of the triangle, with each point representing a stakeholder individual or groups of individuals. Others have created artistic expressions such as a patchwork 'quilt' stamped with handprints. Still others imagine a 'do no harm room furnished with, among other things, comfortable chairs arranged in a circle. These more human images suggest that the core of restorative justice focuses on people. (Walgrave, 2004: 61)

The cultural web is a very promising tool in considering how restorative ideas might be implemented in prisons. It can help to audit the way in which changes are already taking place in some prisons and how more could be achieved through further development of restorative methods and culture. Restorative practitioners who are transforming community based penalties are beginning to work more in prisons and their efforts could be seen through the model of the cultural web so that their projects are focused but also able to influence the wider prison community in a holistic way.

Table 2 illustrates the connecting links between prison processes and the elements of the cultural web. It gives an idea of how important it is to develop ideas in several areas in order to touch on all the elements of the web. In all this, staff management is crucial. The table provides prison managers, restorative practitioners and prison staff with a clear idea of the challenges and opportunities for restorative justice within prison establishments. By way of example, we conclude this chapter with a description of a hypothetical disciplinary process, conducted under restorative principles.

A RESTORATIVE SYSTEM OF BUILDING SOCIAL ORDER

Adjudications as restorative conferences

A disciplinary system that puts restorative principles into practice means a change in traditional patterns. Adjudications play a crucial role in upholding social order inside a prison. But because order is defined from the top down, adjudications also function as the means by which governors defend the prison's authority. The focus is on the rules broken and the proof that the accused is guilty. When the guilty has been identified, then the adjudication centres on fixing an appropriate punishment. The disciplinary 'award' is a demonstration of the governor's power over the prisoner.

	Power structures	Organ. structures	Control systems	Routines and rituals	Myths and stories	Symbols
Induction			•	•		
Complaints and requests	•		•			
Adjudications	•		•	•	•	•
Anti-bullying strategy	•		•	•		
Race relations	•			•		
Violence reduction strategy	•		•		•	•
Resettlement			•	•		•
Offending behaviour			•	•		
External outreach	•	•			•	•
Release circles	•	•			•	
Staff arrangements	•	•	•	•	•	

Table 2: *Identifying areas of impact on the cultural web*

To reconsider the aim of securing social order from the perspective of restorative justice, we need to build on the basic values of healing, voluntary participation, respect, empowerment, inclusiveness, equal status, personal accountability and problem-solving.

If this is the heart of restorative justice, then how would a restorative approach transform the way prisons maintain social order and personal responsibility? Here, we refer to the most fitting restorative framework available, which (depending on the situation) could be mediation, a conference, a circle, a panel of peers or some other forum.

Let's say a prisoner is stopped by an officer and found to be in possession of another inmate's phonecard. In the normal run of events, he would be charged with unauthorised possession and taken before the governor in an adjudication. Tracing the ways a traditional adjudication versus a restorative system might deal with this situation will provide a concrete example of different power structures, rituals, stories and symbols: it will illustrate a cultural web of restorative justice in a prison.

The traditional adjudication tends to value coercion and separation. The practical outcomes of adjudications are often segregation; so that either they are imposed as a punishment, or the offender is separated from the victim in the interests of restoring order. Segregation does not solve the problem between the victim and the perpetrator. Indeed, it may make the victim's situation worse.

imposed as a punishment, or the offender is separated from the victim in the interests of restoring order. Segregation does not solve the problem between the victim and the perpetrator. Indeed, it may make the victim's situation worse.

Restorative justice holds that a direct encounter between victim and offender is preferable, provided both parties are willing. We can imagine a direct meeting in the prison between the person who committed the harm and the one most directly harmed by it. These two people are privileged, in that they are best-placed to understand exactly what happened, and therefore best-equipped to decide how one person can make amends to the other. (That, and not punishment or power over prisoners, is what a restorative approach to rebuilding social order is all about.)

Restorative processes in this case are set in motion by three people: the officer who acts on behalf of the prison community to ensure safety; the prisoner whose phonecard was taken (the victim); and the person who committed the harm. If either of the prisoners decides they do not want to try restorative justice, then by default they have decided to deal with the problem through the disciplinary system. If they decide in this way, their first choice (exercising control over the process by rejecting the chance at restorative justice) is also their last. From then on, the disciplinary process, following prison's hierarchical structure, is managed by the officer, senior officers and then the Governor.

A restorative process brings people together, in that the outcome is ideally decided in a dialogue between the offender and the victim (and often the supporters of each party). The response is inherently collaborative. It is clear from the research evidence that restorative justice works best when the agreements about how to respond to a conflict are developed by the input of both parties and when both parties personally commit themselves to living up to their part in the agreement. Restorative outcomes are not likely to succeed if they are imposed on the offender by the facilitator.

But we need to begin with the person who was robbed. A restorative response will focus on the harms suffered rather than the rule broken. The initial aim of a restorative response is to discover who was harmed, and how they were harmed. It necessarily involves the harmed person. Indeed, they have a central role in the process.

The procedure is intended to fulfil the victim's needs. Hence, how the process goes, and above all, the solutions to the problem that are agreed are largely dependent on the victim. Nonetheless, one restorative justice approach, a scripted conference, is carefully structured to avoid putting too much stress on victims. Victims and offenders also hold the power to decide on how much they wish to participate throughout the process.

The victim is asked questions about what happened and what impact that had had on him. This process empowers the victim more than the present system, but because victims are often made to feel weak by the damage done to them, the restorative justice response goes further. As the process develops, they might be asked for their views on how the wrongs could be made right. But they do not have to make suggestions about how the perpetrator, the responsible person, can make amends if they don't want to. The meeting might become a forum for putting together a support package to ensure that the victim's needs arising from the harm will be met in the future.

What about the prisoner who committed the robbery? The disciplinary system defines him as a prisoner who has broken, or rebelled against, the rules. The perpetrator's role in the adjudication is to accept the Governor's decision on the evidence, and to take the punishment imposed by the Governor.

Restorative justice works on a different basis of personal responsibility for one's actions. A restorative approach is based on the idea that the prisoner has a central role in deciding how to solve the problem caused by his behaviour. The prisoner who took the phonecard was responsible for setting the process in motion, but he is also responsible in the sense of being personally accountable to the person he robbed for the harm he has committed. Finally, he is treated as a responsible person in that he is given the opportunity to make amends for the damage he has done.

The restorative process will uphold and support the perpetrator of harm as a person while condemning his or her actions. The main aim is to enlist their cooperation in the pursuit of making things right again. This is not easy to do.

The facilitation of restorative justice responses is intended to show offenders, from the very start, that their presence and input is valued; that their version of events is honoured and heard; and that the process expects them to respond in a responsible and respectful manner.

It is possible that, in the emotional atmosphere of a restorative conference, an offender might be motivated to promise more than can reasonably be expected. Thus, these meetings also provide the support that offenders need to fulfil their obligations. To expect them to make amends for the harm they have inflicted is empowering. But fatalism and a sense of worthlessness can creep in if they find themselves incapable of completing their side of the agreement. Hence, one role of the facilitators is to judge the extent to which the terms of the agreement are realistically achievable by the offender, and whether the terms are needlessly punitive.

Power in restorative responses to harmful behaviour

Now that we have traced a typical restorative process, we can draw out some of its main features. For example, what does this suggest about the influence of power in how social order is restored?

The traditional disciplinary system concentrates power and control (and responsibility) at the top. Initially the prisoner who commits the robbery holds the power in the situation, as he can decide whether or not to take his fellow prisoner's property. When the officer stops the prisoner, she asserts control over the situation. The prisoner can have very little impact then on whether he is going to be charged. When the prison officer takes the prisoner to the adjudication, the power shifts to the Governor, who hears the evidence, decides on guilt and on the fitting punishment. With each step, the power controlling the outcome moves up a level in the hierarchy. Ultimately, the decision on how to deal with the problem—the robbery of a prisoner's phonecard—rests with the Governor.

In restorative processes, e.g., a conference or mediation, the structured process helps to lessen any power disparities between individual parties. This different perspective on power means that people in prison who are prepared to give restorative justice a go need to prepare themselves to give greater control over the outcome to the people who are directly involved in the problem. If the prisoners who were directly involved in the robbery decide to pursue the restorative option, their power over the situation is maintained right through the process.

The victim would normally have little role in an adjudication following the discovery of his phonecard in the possession of another prisoner. The role of victims in the restorative process is very different, because they have the power from the start to decide whether to pursue restorative justice. If so, they can gain choices about the kind of restorative approach to be used. But it is in the meeting (either directly with the perpetrator, or indirectly through a mediator) that victims hold onto the most significant power over the situation. There, they exercise power in the way they choose to characterise the harm they have experienced, and in their thoughts about what they want to happen in the future.

There is an obvious contrast between these victims' perceptions of the problem on one hand and the way the situation is defined when it comes under prison discipline. And that contrast signals the shift of power over the situation, from the prison hierarchy to the victim, that is, to the person who was most directly harmed by the robbery.

In restorative approaches, the person who committed the harm (the perpetrator of the robbery) will be encouraged to take responsibility for the harm done. There are at least three steps to 'taking responsibility'. First, their decision to try a restorative process is not sufficient: they must also accept responsibility for the harm caused. Although accepting responsibility sounds more like a burden than a power, the alternative is a fatalistic attitude to one's own actions, the ultimate sense of being powerless.

The second way of encouraging personal responsibility is that restorative justice processes show the perpetrator that he holds the power to resolve the problem he has caused. The opportunity to make amends gives the perpetrator another power that is also denied him by the disciplinary process.

Third, actually carrying out the agreement, making a concrete demonstration of personal responsibility, may lead the offender to increased victim empathy. He holds onto the power to make amends long after the restorative forum, as he fulfils his side of the agreement.

The effectiveness of restorative justice processes depends on ensuring that the power to resolve the problem rests with the two prisoners most directly involved. The role of the facilitator is not to control the process, but to facilitate: literally to enable the process to happen by guiding the participants and (to a lesser extent) making sure people show respect for each other. The facilitator is not meant to be holding the power in the conference (in contrast to the role of a Governor in adjudications).

This example shows that when restorative justice is brought to bear on a problem situation, its use has dramatic implications for the normal power structure in the prison. (Note that in the disciplinary process, the Governor holds power over the situation; in contrast, our discussion of how a robbery might be handled through restorative justice did not mention a Governor.)

The role of the wider prison community

Many conferences involve others who have been affected by the actions of the perpetrator. Other prisoners may have an interest in how the problem is resolved; prison officers also have a stake in maintaining a safe and peaceful prison environment. Therefore others are also encouraged to exercise their power through the restorative process. For example, the officer who confronted the perpetrator initially exercised her power over the perpetrator by initiating the restorative conference. She might turn to the trained restorative justice coordinator to pick up the case. But that would not be the end of her involvement in the problem situation.

If the method of dealing with the incident is a conference, it would be likely that the officer would be asked to attend, so that the conference could benefit by hearing her perspective. Although this sounds like she would be giving evidence, in a similar role to the one she would have performed in an adjudication, the nature of her involvement in a restorative conference would be very different.

In an adjudication, her role would be limited to reading out the evidence and (sometimes) replying to questions put to her by the Governor. In most restorative justice mediation or conferences, the officer would be asked to describe how the responsible person's actions had affected her. She might also take on the role of a supporter and make suggestions about how the problem could be resolved.

Her role would be much more personal than in an adjudication. In a conference, the officer's official powers would be set aside. Being a prison officer does not mean that she would have the authority to determine how the conference was conducted. But her actual influence on the conference process and the outcome could be much greater than would be possible in adjudications.

Outcomes

The longer term goal is to enable both parties to live together without further recriminations, to bring to an end the costly cycles of revenge and retaliation. This does not mean that the two parties are expected to become friends. If the situation that leads to a restorative response involves the bullying of one person by another, the agreement might require the offender to avoid coming into contact with the victim. Separation which is maintained by both parties (not imposed from above) might be the best solution to the harms caused by a bullying relationship. Nonetheless, what is important here is the principle that the separation in this case would be based on the terms which the two parties directly involved created, agreed upon, and to which each was personally committed.

The strength (or benefit) of restorative justice when used to deal with harmful behaviour in prison is that the flat power structure encourages the people who have harmed others to take responsibility for their actions and this may lead them to understand that they, too, have a stake in creating a safe and orderly prison community. The restorative approach also means that the solutions to the problem will be more likely to bring about the desired changes than a disciplinary award, because the solution has been devised by the people who are directly involved in the problem.

Prisons should not expect too much of restorative justice. Properly done, it is demanding of staff time. Thus, restorative responses will require much greater support for both offenders and victims than is given by the current system. Any restorative approach, as a response to a hurtful event, highlights deep human needs. It is not the role of a conference, mediation, or meeting to fulfil all of these human needs. Rather, in making a commitment to a restorative approach, the prison also commits itself to empowering prisoners to create legitimate ways of getting their basic human needs met.

CHAPTER 4

Resistance to Change

CONFLICTING PARADIGMS

Prisons are complex institutions. Inevitably, there are aspects of prisons that welcome restorative justice, and others that stand in opposition to it. An image might help to flag up the approach we wish to take in this chapter. Imagine two prisons — one is coercive, dehumanising and degrading; the other works with prisoners in a reforming, problem-solving and reintegrating mission.

The first prison can be summed up in a quote from 30 years ago:

> We submit that the basic evils of imprisonment are that it denies autonomy, degrades dignity, impairs or destroys self-reliance, inculcates authoritarian values, minimizes the likelihood of beneficial interaction with one's peers, fractures family ties, destroys the family's economic stability, and prejudices the prisoner's future prospects for any improvement in his economic and social status.
>
> (American Friends Service Committee, 1972: 33)

In the punitive prison, the aims are to exclude, humiliate and harm people who have broken the law. In this prison, coercive and stigmatising controls, separation from the support of loved ones, and domination and brutality degrade prisoners and staff. For offenders, time inside will increase the risk of re-offending on release.

The second prison is dedicated to respecting human dignity, and works on the principle that wrongdoing creates an obligation to make amends. It understands that crime reflects and causes social conflicts that need to be managed. The prison provides a place of safety in which all those affected by a crime can work together to reach a consensus about how to resolve the problems the crime has left in its wake. In the second prison, people are provided with a support structure, caring staff and opportunities to enable them to address the problems that led them into crime. The emphasis is on preparing the ground for release, ensuring that a proper network of care is in place to help the person to a successful resettlement.

There is a sting in this tale. The two prisons are the same place; or, more accurately, these two images coexist in every prison in England and Wales. They symbolise what prisons are and do. The most restorative prisons in this country (Grendon and Send are two examples) nonetheless shatter family ties, undermine a person's sense of self-worth, and brand them with the stigma of time spent in prison. The harshest, most punitive prisons (like Armley in Leeds or Wandsworth), under intense pressure of numbers, nonetheless show genuine compassion by the ways they support prisoners, such as the suicide prevention work in Leeds and Radio Wanno in Wandsworth.

There are strongly held values in prisons that make it very difficult for the prison to put restorative justice into practice. In every prison, there are also values which would be supportive of all that restorative justice hopes to achieve for offenders, for victims of crime, and for the wider society. Our purpose in this chapter is to anticipate the ways in which conventional prison culture will find it difficult to accommodate restorative justice and to spell out explicitly some of the points at which prisons might resist the implications of restorative justice.

Table 3 presents some of the main differences between the philosophy that guides imprisonment and restorative justice.

Table 3: *Prison culture and restorative values*

Punitive values	Restorative values
Punishing	Healing
Control and dominate prisoners	Empower people
Exclude, separate	Include, participate
Stigmatise as untrustworthy	Respect
Treat the guilty as passive	Expect personal accountability
Security based on superior power	Order based on negotiating conflicts
Regimentation	Honouring individuality

The experience of imprisonment ...

- is shameful, leading to or confirming low self-esteem;
- is dangerous, reinforcing attitudes that produce criminal behaviour; and
- causes measurable damage that increases the likelihood of re-offending.

Power domination, exclusion and stigmatisation might be said to be fundamental to the institution of imprisonment. Prisons deliver criminal justice punishment, in part by demonstrating the total domination of the state over the offender.

In criminal justice systems, imprisonment comes after a legal authority judges the offender to be guilty; then decides on the amount of pain that is required in retribution; and then imposes the punishment on the offender. The routines and rituals of criminal justice, its organizational structure and its power structures maintain a passive image of offenders. Criminal justice punishment is enacted by the state upon prisoners—the prisoners' role is to accept their punishment.

The title 'National Offender Management Service' that now covers prisons and probation implies that offenders are impersonal units to be 'managed'. The principle of control suggests that, in order to function smoothly, prisons must deny prisoners the right to make decisions. Staff must remain in control at all times, and for this to happen, they cannot risk giving prisoners a say in how the prison is run.

Stating this point in terms of concrete examples: when prisons ...

- tell prisoners what time they must get out of bed;
- assign jobs on the basis of who conforms;
- enforce limited options in diet, apparel, job opportunities, location of one's bed;
- stipulate one set of rules for prisoners and a different set for staff;
- regulate contact with families and friends, for example by making telephones accessible only at set times; or
- require prisoners to submit to any practice that does not occur outside (e.g., random drug tests) ...

when prisons treat offenders like this, they inflict harm as they demonstrate the dominance of the state over the offender.

Such coercive practices are damaging. Routines and policies that are intended to dominate prisoners, stigmatise, condemn them as untrustworthy, and inhibit their self-determination are likely to institutionalise and disempower them. This has negative implications for tackling re-offending. In her recent book on prison culture, Alison Liebling wrote:

> What we see in our work ... is an empirical reminder that human beings yearn to be in social environments which contain certain *virtues* (like fairness and respect ...) and that the experience of being in punitive and disrespectful environments is traumatic and damaging. (Liebling, 2004: 166)

One of the ways current prison practice degrades dignity is stigmatisation. Prisons, especially in the public sector, consistently treat offenders as fundamentally defective. Prison management and staff are accustomed to making decisions that have a profound impact of the prisoner's life without consulting the individual prisoner. In this regard, prisons reinforce the branding of offenders that begins far earlier in the criminal justice process.

The principles of separation and exclusion inhibit personal accountability. Prisons are not welcoming towards victims—it is an open question whether the wall is intended to keep prisoners in or the community out. Keeping out victims of crime means that prisoners are shielded from knowing how their behaviour has affected others.

Prisoners are aware of the attitude of staff. They are quick to pick up on signs of disrespect, or that officers consider it part of their duty to impose punishment. Liebling drew a link between the officers' control functions and the prisoners' perception of prison as a punitive environment:

> Prisoners felt most strongly about being locked up for long periods of time; staff having so much power over them; and staff attitudes ... Many prisoners experienced imprisonment as deeply punishing:
> 'My feeling is that it's punishment. It seems as if everything is to make you suffer. Everything is done as punishment. It's mental torture. I *feel* it as a punishment, even though I'm on remand. They drain people, make it feel bad ... They shouldn't be so heavy-handed—they do it with an attitude'. (Liebling, 2004: 135)

It is worth stating that not all of the cultural resistance to restorative justice comes from staff and management. Prisoners, too, can find restorative values such as empowerment, personal responsibility, inclusion and voluntarism hard to accept. Advocates of restorative processes need to win over prisoners, as well as governors and officers. We need to be aware that the ethos of prisoners on the wing will evoke considerable resistance to accepting personal responsibility for harms caused.

Prison culture and the restorative ethos

The foregoing helps to identify the likely obstacles that traditional prison culture can put in the way of the proper development of restorative justice.

Restorative justice seeks first to put right the harms caused by criminal acts. The punitive prison is a reaction to an original harm that piles on the damage, spreading it from the crime, to the people who must work in prisons, those who are confined there, their families and their futures.

Although prisons are about domination and segregation, they also accommodate efforts at rehabilitation. They provide a structured environment and staff support prisoners with help and advice. It is possible to identify more positive values in prisons. A space can be found for restorative values by exploring these positive aspects of prisons and building on the common ground.

Empowerment calls for systems to give people opportunities to make decisions that will determine their future. Inclusion means that decisions are more practical and responsive to the basic needs of prisoners if they have had input into the decision-making process. In restorative justice, the value of inclusiveness encourages the offender to take personal responsibility for the harm he or she caused.

Restorative justice works best when the people directly involved in a crime are empowered to decide how the problems the crime caused can be solved or healed. Prisons regiment prisoners as a way of getting through the day with a minimum of fuss. By controlling their movements and activities, prisons deny autonomy and degrade dignity. Is it possible to imagine a prison in which the goal was to enable each prisoner to exercise choice at every hour of the day about how their time could be used to fulfil their potential?

Two of the core principles of restorative justice hold: (i) that the response to crime should be first about healing the harm done; and (ii) that the process of reintegration must be built on empowering the offender to take responsibility for making amends. The value restorative justice gives to the empowerment of the offender implies that prisons must be transformed, so that they cease to symbolise (and practise) the state's total power over offenders.

The value restorative justice places on personal accountability implies that part of the core tasks of prison officers should be to encourage prisoners to spend their time on making amends to their victims (provided the victim is willing) or indirectly, to society (if their victim does not wish to receive direct reparation.) At the very least, the prisoner should recognise that he or she owes a duty to their victim, even if no face-to-face encounter is possible.

Prisons strive for a safe environment. But it is obvious that they are not safe. As the American Friends Service Committee stated, prison 'minimizes the likelihood of beneficial interaction with one's peers'. Prison staff cannot guarantee personal safety, and so prisoners must look out for their own safety in a society where the risks of being assaulted, having one's property taken or being exploited in other ways are very high.

Restorative justice invests a great deal of energy and expertise in building a trusting and safe setting, where people involved in a conflict feel that they can share their feelings openly without risk of being humiliated. Restorative prisons are designed to enhance offenders' self-esteem through opportunities for self-determination (empowerment). Such prisons expect prisoners to contribute voluntarily to the life of the prison community. Inclusiveness means that the person is engaged in all decisions made about their time in prison.

WHAT MATTERS IN PRISON

Hans Toch (1992) listed seven basic needs of prisoners: privacy, safety, structure, support, emotional feedback, activity and freedom. Prisoners need support and emotional feedback to feel as though they are being treated as individual, and human, rather than units to be managed. They need both structure, to organize their day, and activity, in the sense of opportunities to interact and spend their time in meaningful and personally fulfilling ways. Toch added that different groups of prisoners prioritise these needs in different ways. For example, a younger group would sacrifice some security to gain greater activity; whereas an older group might favour structure, privacy and safety over relative freedom.

Liebling's work revealed a different set of values, based on interviews with prisoners and staff in which she asked them to specify what really mattered to them in prison. The list they came up with included: respect, humanity, trust, support, fairness, order, safety, well-being, personal development, decency, social life and meaning.

These values bring humanity and a positive vision to the principles of segregation, dominance and punishment. The impetus in prisons to maintain control and enforce separation remains, but it is tempered by the importance given to respect, trust, emotional feedback and privacy. Indeed, no prison could run – no prison community could survive – if it did not recognise the needs and values espoused by Liebling and Toch.

These are not 'pie-in-the-sky' hopes of the positive ideals that could have a future impact on the way prisons are run. Liebling's interviews and analyses showed that people who live and work in prisons value respect, trust, fairness, safety and decency. The challenge is to build on this value base, so that the restorative values become the norm for prison staff.

Liebling applied to prisons a theory of political values developed by Valerie Braithwaite. According to Braithwaite, societies run on two different sets of values: security values, which are about stability and order, and harmony values, which are about peaceful co-existence and co-operation. The two sets of values can be laid out as follows:

Security values	Harmony values
Self-protection	Peaceful co-existence
Rule of law	Mutual respect, human dignity
Authority	Sharing of resources
Competitiveness	Development of individual potential
Tough law enforcement	Wealth redistribution

(Liebling: 438)

It might appear that prisons are all about security values; that, by their nature, prisons fail to honour harmony values. That would be a mistaken interpretation. Liebling contended that every establishment sets a balance between the two, so that some prisons give greater weight to harmony values than others.

She added that problems are caused by emphasising security at the cost of harmony:

> Braithwaite and colleagues show how punitive and stigmatizing (disrespectful, degrading, or outcasting) punishments, arising from a security orientation, threaten the individual and may lead to destructive forms of shame, and rage ... Defensive strategies follow, which deflect 'blame' on to others. Disrespect begets disrespect ... Too great a preoccupation with security reduces legitimacy and perceptions of fairness. (Liebling, 2004: 441)

Valerie Braithwaite's scheme recognised broader dimensions of community life, such as competition, resources, dignity and desires for self-protection or wealth redistribution. Her analysis also made clear that social order depends on striking the right balance between the two sets of values. Prisons need to maintain security in the sense of honouring the needs for self-protection, recognising the reality of competition and defending their authority. But if management and policies define the officer-prisoner relationship in competitive, antagonistic terms, the weight given to security values will sustain disruption, conflict and disorder in the prison community. Prisons need to honour the values of mutual respect, peaceful co-existence and individual development as a means of securing social order.

Liebling doubted the capacity of prisons to base their culture primarily upon harmony values. The obstacle, as she saw it, was power. Prisons are places of domination. Although in theory the two sets of principles should be balanced, she seems to be saying that prisons will always favour security:

> Whilst this morally balanced approach to law-breaking behaviour in general is inherently limited in the prison (for the prison constitutes a place of domination), this analysis, and the understanding of the effects of degradation it allows, supports our case that the prison is a morally dangerous environment. It is dangerous precisely because of the need for force to be used and security to be accomplished. Because power is corruptible, and security values inherently involve scepticism and detachment, it is extraordinarily difficult to pursue respect and security values simultaneously. (Liebling: 442)

Her words should be a constant reminder that prisons can be a hostile environment in which to develop restorative justice. Nonetheless, prisons still have great potential to bring out the best in people. Prisons still demonstrate that human beings can reach out to each other across the divides of uniform and dominance. Coercion is woven into the fabric of the prison's power structures, but to characterise relationships by this dimension alone ignores the real, human world of prisons, in which, for example:

- a prisoner can be seen putting her arm around the shoulders of an officer who was recently bereaved;
- an officer tells a young prisoner, 'Good luck in your exam,' and means it;
- an adjudicating governor asks a prisoner who has been found to have taken cannabis what he thinks the governor should do;
- a senior officer calls a group of prisoners together to discuss what should be done about a recent spate of cell thefts; and
- a night duty officer sits talking quietly with a young man who is very depressed.

These human interactions provide anecdotal evidence that prison life does not have to be defined by harm (punishment) and power (domination). Prisons practise both the harmony and the security sets of values. There is a fine balance in Liebling's work, as she recognised that prisons cannot maintain social order if they ignore the harmony values. Anyone who sees prisons as inherently oppressive ignores the mutual respect (albeit at only a basic level) which enables a prison officer and a prisoner to negotiate a dispute safely. Anyone who believes that prisons are run purely on coercion has failed to notice the opportunities prisoners take to create their own sense of order.

The choices by which managers and officers set the balance between security and harmony in their establishment help to determine the paradigm for securing social order. Focusing on the problem of social order can illustrate further tensions between prison culture and restorative culture. But this concern can also lead us to imagine ways in which restorative values can complement the prison's efforts to instil a sense of community, tolerance, and cooperation.

VALUES, RESTORATIVE JUSTICE AND CONFLICT

Social order and violence are perennial problems in prisons. The risk of fights and assaults varies widely between prisons. But in every prison, violent incidents threaten to undermine the smooth running of the establishment. Prisoners cannot work on offending behaviour or contribute to the prison community if they live in fear, if there is a serious danger that they will be victimised by other prisoners.

Richard Sparks, Tony Bottoms and Will Hay describe social order as:

> any long-standing pattern of social relations (characterised by a minimum level of respect for persons) in which the expectations that participants have of one another are commonly met, though not necessarily without contestation. Order can also, in

part, be defined negatively as the absence of violence, overt conflict, or the imminent threat of the chaotic breakdown of social routines. (Sparks, *et al.*, 1996: 119)

Two characteristics of social order that are highlighted by their definition are 'a minimum level of respect' and 'the absence of violence'. This section explores what prisons can do to foster respect and reduce violence. It also considers what contribution restorative processes can make to these twin aims, in pursuit of social order.

Exploring the background to a specific fight will bring to light some of the factors that threaten social order in prison[1]. Two prisoners worked together as painters. One, whom we might call 'Eastleigh', was threatened by the other, 'Kennet'. Kennet was irritated because Eastleigh did not do his share of the work. When Kennet complained to Eastleigh, Eastleigh threatened to hit him. The next day Kennet complained again, and threats were exchanged. Kennet tried to hit Eastleigh with a broom, but Eastleigh punched Kennet's face and knocked him to the floor. Officers moved in and forced the two apart.

Both prisoners were sensitive to their perceptions that the other person was trying to dominate them.

Eastleigh said: 'He was deliberately niggling, a natural bully.' He added: 'Once you allow someone to push you about, you've got troubles. If they realise you're weak, they'll pick on you all the time.'

Kennet said: 'I'm not his lackey. If he's going to take on a job, he should do it. If not, sit in his cell. He was expecting me to do his work for him.'

They also explained that their argument was influenced by the fact that they were in prison at the time.

Kennet said: 'He'd have got the sack from his job outside.'

Kennet focused on the ways that prison social structure assigns good jobs to prisoners who conform, whether or not they work hard.

Eastleigh said the dispute was aggravated: '... Because you're bunched up together. The atmosphere in prison causes fights. You can't put that many men together without some sort of friction.'

Eastleigh's point draws attention to a central challenge facing prison managers: there are perverse cycles of violence, in which distrust and actual dangers encourage prisoners to think they need to use violence to defend themselves, and thus the risks of fights and assaults, and the seriousness of such incidents, escalate.

We are not suggesting that every prison is violent. But the example provided by this incident shows, following the definition by Sparks *et al.* how violence can disturb social order. When fights and assault are commonplace and prisoners have learned to expect violence from each other, it is clear that social order has broken down.

In most prisons, fights and assaults constitute an occasional break in the social order. Whether the prison is one in which violence is endemic, or a less frequent event that disturbs the social order, the question remains: How can

---

[1] This incident, and the conflict-centred analysis that is used to explain it, came from Kimmett's research, sponsored by the Economic and Social Research Council, published in Edgar, O'Donnell, and Martin (2003).

prison management, staff and prisoners work together to build social order, promote a safe environment, and make trust and respect the expectation each member of the community has of every other one?

A conflict-centred approach to reducing violence builds on the recognition that prisons generate conflict. The institutional structure of prisons creates conflicts, between prisoners and managers, between managers and staff, and among prisoners. Attention to the conflict-generating dynamics of prisons (the conflict-centred approach) provides an effective foundation for strategies to reduce violence.

The distinctions between conflict and violence are crucial. Conflict can be understood as a clash of interests, competing needs, or antagonistic behaviour. When violence occurs, it is often the outcome of a conflict. However, conflict is an essential part of a dynamic social order, providing energy to any organization. The answer to violence is not to have no conflict (because that is impossible when people have to live together). Rather, it is to manage conflicts so that the outcome doesn't involve intentionally harming the other person.

The deprivations that create conflict

Four aspects of the typical prison help to show how these institutions promote conflicts. They are:

- the deprivation of material goods;
- the high risk of victimisation;
- the loss of personal autonomy; and
- the lack of nonviolent routes for resolving conflicts

Prisons control people's access to resources. A graphic image of the way that the prison environment can create conflict is the wing telephone. Prisons deny family members the opportunity to have continuous contact with their fathers, sons, brothers, or daughters, wives, partners. In the evenings, about 40-60 people must share three pay telephones. The inevitable queues, the informal deals for phonecards, the impatience of waiting and the desperation of wanting to stay on the phone all give rise to disputes between prisoners. By restricting access to the telephone, prisons cause prisoners to compete for a scarce resource.

The second structural source of conflict is the risk of being victimised by other prisoners. Gresham Sykes summed up the feelings of many prisoners when he wrote:

> While it is true that every prisoner does not live in the constant fear of being robbed or beaten, the constant companionship of thieves, rapists, murderers and aggressive homosexuals is far from reassuring. (Sykes, 1959: 77)

There is a perverse cycle in prisons, when prisoners fear being assaulted and gain the will to defend themselves by force if necessary. A prisoner commits an assault because he fears that he will be assaulted or robbed unless he demonstrates his toughness. As a result, the risk of assault in the prison community increases. Actions motivated by a desire for personal safety make the prison more threatening and dangerous for everyone.

The third source of conflict is the deprivation of personal power or self-determination. Erving Goffman described prisons as an 'echelon society', meaning that prisoners are at the bottom of a rigid hierarchy of power (1961). The actions of any prisoner are subject to the scrutiny and judgement of any member of staff. With their autonomy so restricted, prisoners become sensitive to the balance of power between them and other prisoners. Wary of being seen as weak, they perceive a need to stand up for themselves and are quick to stand up to perceived slights.

The fourth factor is a lack of opportunities available to prisoners to resolve their conflicts non-violently. In part, we refer to the relative lack of wing forums, impartial mediators who are trained to intervene in disputes, and opportunities to negotiate win-win solutions.

Some kind of forum to enable prisoners to discuss and resolve their differences is a vital alternative to the tradition of settling differences by fighting. Governors and staff are deeply mistaken if they believe that prisoners fight because they have volatile personalities or that the prisoner culture uncritically supports a violent code. These assumptions are empty excuses to do nothing about the social structure that generates conflict, while placing the blame for fights and assaults fully on the prisoners involved.

Prison Reform Trusts's (PRT) study of prisoner councils brought to light the importance of providing a safety valve for tensions. In one establishment, the management strongly believed that their council had led to a reduction in violence. A prisoner interviewed in a different establishment described the contrast he saw between prisons that had, or lacked, a council:

> You get anger in other prisons. You walk past another con and you feel the anger welling up. Soon you feel that with every other prisoner. You feel the tension all of the time. Here, you bring it up in the wing meeting, and settle it. (PRT, 2004: 25)

SOCIAL ORDER IN PRISON

Following the pattern set by this analysis of the sources of prison conflict, it makes sense that social order can be established and sustained by tackling these four dimensions:

- fulfilling prisoners' basic human needs;
- working to ensure personal safety;
- providing opportunities to exercise personal autonomy; and
- building in mechanisms for prisoners to resolve conflicts.

The first step in building a sustainable social order is to consult with prisoners to identify the needs that the prison is failing to meet. John Burton asks the question:

> Do we assume that conflicts are due to human aggressiveness requiring and justifying authoritarian political structures and processes of punishment and containment as the means by which to control conflict; or do we assume that there are inherent human needs which, if not satisfied, lead to conflictual behaviors? (Burton 1990: 29)

Following Burton's insight, the first step in building a sustainable social order is to understand violence as a result of the frustration of basic human needs. It follows that there is enormous potential for building sustainable social order when managers and staff are open to exploring with prisoners the basic human needs that the prison is failing to meet. As we have seen, Hans Toch listed privacy, safety, structure, support, emotional feedback, activity and freedom as prisoners' basic needs (1992: 21-22). A vital part of building social order is consulting prisoners about which needs the prison must work towards fulfilling.

The second part of the strategy must be to empower officers to ensure safety from victimisation. Much of the victimisation that occurs — including threats of violence, thefts and assault — is criminal. That so much victimisation occurs is evidence that prisons are failing to keep people safe in custody. Typically, a dispute between prisoners escalates, from insults and mutual threats, to pushing and shoving, and then an all-out fight. Eastleigh and Kennet had been exchanging threats for days before their argument erupted in physical violence.

The typical build-up to a violent incident demonstrates that much violence could be prevented by proper training of officers. Officers could be taught how to spot volatile disputes early, before they have escalated into open fighting. Training could also teach them when and how to intervene, to give them confidence in mediating to resolve conflicts between prisoners.

The benefits of providing opportunities to exercise personal autonomy were central to the success of the Barlinnie Unit. David J Cooke described the theory on which the unit was based:

> This Unit was established in 1972 because of concerns about the increasing level of violence in Scottish prisons. A radical approach was adopted. The regime plan was based on three underlying principles: first, the need to reduce the traditional hostility between staff and prisoners; second, the need to increase the autonomy of prisoners; and third, the need to provide a forum in which feelings of anger, hostility and frustration could be expressed and conflicts resolved. (Cooke, 1992: 2)

Equally, the Prison Reform Trust study on prisoner councils (PRT, 2004) found that these bodies transformed the community by establishing a proper forum in which conflicts could be aired and worked on. Councils increased the managers' awareness of where the regime caused hardships for prisoners. But they also greatly improved the relationships between management, staff and prisoners. The inclusive approach embodied in councils demonstrated to prisoners that their needs were important. Moreover, it proved to them that their perspective and input were valued.

Hence, the conflict-centred approach is pro-active and multi-faceted, allowing steps to be taken early, so that violence can be prevented. Managers and officers can identify aspects of the social setting (such as the arrangements for supervising the painting work) which could be re-organized to reduce the sources of conflict. It would certainly mean working with prisoners like Kennet and Eastleigh to develop in them better techniques of handling situations of conflict. When Eastleigh and Kennet became aware of conflicting interests they could have been offered the option of taking the dispute to mediation, and perhaps reach an agreement that would meet both sets of interests.

Timing is crucial. A restorative conference could have been brought in to work with Kennet and Eastleigh after the fight to clear the air. They could both benefit from an opportunity to describe how the incident affected them, what their feelings were as the dispute grew, and what they would like to see done in future to prevent further violence. But it would be better if a pro-active intervention, focused on mediation, had been available before the clash of interests led to mutual threats and accusations.

Restorative justice and conflict resolution

The influence of restorative justice on social order in prison depends on the extent of commitment to restorative values by governors and senior management teams. There is a wealth of restorative processes available, but prison staff need to be open to working with them.

Different threats to stability and harmony require different approaches. A brief list of restorative processes here will be followed, in *Chapter 5*, with more detailed descriptions of each method.

At the heart of restorative justice are processes devoted to building consensus among the people most directly involved in criminal events: victim-offender mediation and conferences. More widely, under the restorative justice umbrella, there are processes designed to facilitate the input of stakeholders into decisions about the aftermath of a crime. Examples include youth panels, sentencing circles, and circles of support and accountability. Work with offenders, such as that done by the Alternatives to Violence Project, the Inside Out Trust and the Sycamore Tree Project, focus on transforming the perspective of the prisoner and are restorative in their ability to empower the offender to make a positive contribution to their community—which can mean that they begin by exercising a constructive influence on the prison community, helping to maintain harmony.

Conflict resolution, mediation and restorative justice are focused on harm, and are effective methods of reducing its after effects on individuals and relationships. Mediation can be brought into play *before* any criminal harm is committed. Restorative justice in criminal justice on one hand, and mediation and conflict resolution on the other, share principles such as empowerment, personal accountability, inclusiveness and voluntarism. They treat participants in these processes impartially. Mediation aims to find win-win solutions without using force. Conflict resolution is a pro-active method, to be used early in a dispute, before a crime occurs and restorative justice becomes necessary.

Distinctions between restorative justice conferences and conflict resolution techniques are not absolute. In some restorative conferences, it becomes clear that there had been some mutual harm leading up to the crime. The background to the offence might have included a conflict between the persons identified as the victim and offender. In some conflicts, making progress towards a win-win settlement requires each party to recognise the harm they have caused and the obligation to make amends.

In pursuing the aim of social order, a restorative prison will make use of the full restorative justice toolkit. The approach used will be chosen because it fits the particular type of conflict occurring. A restorative conference is ideal for restoring order after a fight involving six prisoners. The key opponents can be brought together, with their supporters, in a conference to establish who was harmed, who is responsible for that harm, and what can be done to make amends. Such a conference would be public, in that the number of people precludes a strict rule of confidentiality.

When a prisoner alleges that an officer has been abusive or unfair, mediation is the far preferable response. Resolving such a dispute depends on privacy to enable both parties to be fully open about their perspective.

Conflicts are likely when a prisoner who has been segregated, perhaps for bullying, returns to normal location. These situations would benefit from an adapted form of a circle of support and accountability. A small group of peers could commit themselves to supporting the returning prisoner, and, as a group, confronting them if they slipped back into exploitative ways.

VALUES INHERENT IN PRISON SERVICE POLICIES

Recent policy changes in the Prison Service show a recognition that addressing the sources of conflict is an important part of preventing violence. In May 2004, the Prison Service's Safer Custody Group published its 'Violence Reduction Strategy' (VRS) under Prison Service Order (PSO) 2750, encouraging each prison to develop individually tailored methods to reduce or prevent violence — showing strong parallels with restorative justice. Recalling the image of the two prisons, the damaging prison stigmatises individual prisoners as 'violence-prone', dangerous, and high-risk. In contrast, the approach set out in the VRS reflects the healthy, restorative prison.

Quotations from the VRS are taken from PSO 2750. Its stated purpose is, 'To reduce violence, promote a safe and healthy prison environment and foster a culture of non-violence among all staff and prisoners.'

The VRS sets out to achieve this aim by building a sense of teamwork among everyone who lives and works in prisons; by taking a pro-active approach, focusing on the causes of conflicts between prisoners that escalate into fights and assaults; taking seriously all harmful behaviour; and working for a change in behaviour, rather than trying to prevent assaults by threatening punishment.

Although the order does not mention restorative justice, a quick review of some of the features of the VRS will bring out the similarities.

- Restorative justice promotes an inclusive approach to social problems. The VRS mandates prisons to consult prisoners about how to prevent violence: 'Prisoners must be given the opportunity and guidance to participate in and benefit from the strategy.'

- Restorative justice holds that processes should involve a wide range of stakeholders. The VRS mandates discussions with the local trade unions in agreeing upon the strategy.
- Restorative justice demonstrates the importance of taking seriously the harm that one person does to another. The VRS builds on the awareness that when harm is treated as trivial, it soon escalates into more damaging behaviour: 'The effect of verbal abuse, insults or threats is not under-estimated. Verbal abuse, insults or threats are consistently challenged in a constructive way, acknowledging the need for communication.'
- More important, the hurt caused by violence can be trivialised when violence is defined only in terms of physical injury. The VRS uses a definition that highlights the more subtle ways that people can cause each other pain. Violence is defined as: 'any incident in which a person is abused, threatened, or assaulted. This includes an explicit or implicit challenge to their safety, well-being or health. The resulting harm may be physical, emotional or psychological.'
- Restorative justice calls for a non-stigmatising response to those who inflict harm. The VRS states: 'Personal responsibility for incidents is based on an understanding of the causes, rather than allocating blame.'
- The VRS advocates a response to perpetrators of violence that echoes the aim of restorative justice processes to reintegrate the offender: 'Whilst an assailant is left in no doubt that the behaviour is unacceptable and will not be tolerated, sustained, reasoned change in behaviour rather than retribution is sought.'
- The VRS approach is neatly captured in a statement of its intended impact on the prison community, and individuals:

> By constructively and consistently taking action to prevent violence and promote fairness and decency, prisons can offer a structured environment in which to influence future behaviour, encourage positive communication and develop social skills that assist offenders with rehabilitation.

Thus the primary policy used by the Prison Service to nurture safer prisons contains many core principles of restorative justice.

A similar picture emerges from the suicide prevention strategy. In the previous chapter, we drew attention to the approach preferred in traditional prison culture, which was to concentrate energies on identifying those at risk (through the F2052SH form). It is fair to say that the use of the form varied between different prisons, but there was powerful evidence that the reliance on the F2052SH was failing to prevent self-harm and suicide. In the years since 2000, just over one-quarter of the prisoners who took their lives in custody were on the F2052 register at the time of their death. A method that accurately identifies only one in four people at risk is hardly reliable (JCHR, 2004: 20).

In retrospect, the reliance of the system of control on labelling and targeting particular prisoners had two inherent weaknesses. Targeting particular individuals suggested by implication that the prisoners not on the register were not at risk of suicide. The emphasis on risk prediction suggested that suicide prevention was a specialised technique, and reserved for particular prisoners. It undermined a whole prison approach, one in which the whole community — staff and prisoners — took responsibility for providing support for all prisoners.

The second weakness was that it emphasised identification at the expense of how the prison responded to the person, almost as though it was sufficient in itself to record that an individual was in crisis and therefore at risk.

This is not to say that it is pointless to ask officers to attempt to distinguish between people who are coping well and those who need extra support. However, it is a matter of balance. Identifying who is in a crisis is only the first step; how the prison responds to that person is equally important. Reducing self-harm and suicide in prison depends on treating all prisoners with care and respect — not making a special effort only with those deemed at risk.

This is where recent work by the Safer Custody Group is so valuable. The new strategy, ACCT (Assessment, Care in Custody, Teamwork) has moved on to a more responsive and sensitive approach.

The strategy promotes team working, including good communication, diverse roles and co-operation. More important, the emphasis is on a caring and supportive response to prisoners whose distress might lead them to self-harm. Rather than asking officers to watch at risk prisoners carefully, the ACCT encourages staff to interact with, and most important, listen to, prisoners in crisis. Although there are similarities to the F2052 system, in that the process is begun when an officer (or other staff person) fills out an ACCT Plan, the new focus on how the prison community works with the prisoner shows a completely new understanding of how self-harm and suicide can be controlled.

Following the decision to place the prisoner under the ACCT, a Care and Management Plan is agreed. (There is a shift from the predominance of identification under the F2052SH system to the ACCT focus on follow-up care.) The process that follows is guided by these principles:

- the person at risk should be involved in developing the plan;
- the plan is centred on the individual needs of the person;
- there is a practical focus on the person's problems — but the problem-solving method is based on providing the person with options;
- the first principle of the problem-solving phase is to make links between the person and other people who can help/support them;
- other elements of the strategy include attention to any mental health needs, providing a place of safety, and ensuring that officers are there for the person to listen to their perspective.

There are many ways in which this new strategy resonates with good restorative justice practice:

- future-oriented problem-solving methods;
- building the person's community of care;
- listening to the person's perspective and involving them in decisions; and
- responding to their need for personal safety.

These two examples of key Prison Service policies—violence reduction and suicide prevention—closely parallel the core values of restorative justice. The reason for exploring them in depth is to show how restorative justice principles can come alive in responding to deep problems faced by prisons. There may well be some resistance to restorative justice values in areas of prison life governed by what Liebling referred to as security values. However, when prisons are understood as whole, living communities, putting into practice a wide range of values, there are good grounds for expecting a dialogue between prisons and restorative justice to be mutually respectful and beneficial.

Our discussion of social order has demonstrated that there is much common ground between the value prisons place on stability and social order, and the potential contribution that restorative justice can make. However, even where the organization makes a commitment to develop restorative approaches, hidden value tensions can slow progress. To examine this in more depth, we turn to an example outside the prison.

CULTURAL RESISTANCE WITHIN THE POLICE

The Thames Valley Police Service pioneered the use of restorative justice conferences as a first response to offending, beginning in 1998. Whilst traditional police cautions were formal warnings from an officer to an offender, restorative cautions were based on conferences in which all those with a stake in the offence were invited to come together to provide input into the decisions about how the offender could make amends. But as the evaluation found, introducing restorative justice to the police force required a cultural change. Policing culture included beliefs and practices that had to change in order for the officers to respond to crimes in a restorative way. As Hoyle *et al.* state:

> Restorative cautioning would necessarily involve some accommodation and conflict between two sets of philosophies and practices: the first, restorative justice; the second, established policing. The difficulties of changing entrenched policing practices are known to be immense ... Suffice to say that we expected to find that established policing attitudes, structures and patterns of behaviour would shape and often distort the intended restorative nature of cautioning sessions.
>
> (Hoyle *et al.*, 2002: 10)

This is a vitally important observation for our purposes here. Hoyle and her Oxford colleagues expected that introducing restorative practices into a traditional criminal justice culture would come up against resistance and misunderstandings primarily because the 'philosophies and practices' are very different.

The Oxford University evaluation team found strong evidence that the implementation of restorative conferences was flawed in the specific sense that the police facilitators too often slipped into the model of the police investigator. These conferences failed to empower the direct parties to the criminal event.

There was confusion about the intended lines of accountability in the conference. The Oxford team observed a tendency 'for the facilitator to behave as if the offender had to account to him or her personally, with the other participants reduced to little more than passive observers' (Hoyle, *et al.* 2002: 13).

The key word is 'passive' as it highlights that the criminal justice system denies victims and offenders a voice, and takes from them the power to make decisions about what to do to make the situation better. Indeed, these conferences sustained the culture of the criminal justice system in disempowering victims: 'The fact that 38 per cent of victims in the full evaluation were not asked what they would like to come out of the restorative conference is a significant failing' (Hoyle, *et al.* 2002: 14).

What does the Thames Valley example imply about how restorative justice might be developed in prisons? It means that restorative processes are available as a useful option to deal effectively with conflicts (including those between staff and prisoners and between prisoners and other prisoners; but also conflicts between staff and management, between opposing groups within staff, and between an individual prison and national policy). With regard to the day-to-day operations of the prison, restorative practices can function well while focused on bringing solutions to the damaging person-to-person interactions that threaten social cohesion. However, when the restorative process option is exercised, the power structure must change.

Restorative justice brings with it a radically different concept of power, which challenges all parties to change their routine ways of dealing with trouble when it arises. Prison management need to accept that their role is to facilitate the restorative process; and to do this they must cede control over the outcomes to the parties directly involved in the conflict. Prisoners entering into the restorative process must shoulder the burden of personal responsibility that goes with their new capacity to influence policy decisions that are taken. Officers and managers who become involved in restorative processes need to recognise that, within the restorative process, they have no claim to a higher status and might therefore be held accountable to prisoners.

Barbara Toews, of the Pennsylvania Prison Society, set out to develop a new restorative programme in prison by asking the prisoners what they needed to make the philosophy a reality in their prison. Here is what they came up with:

- invite incarcerated men and women into dialogue to learn about their experiences and needs, to elicit their insight on the resources and programmes they need, and to secure their involvement in resource development;
- provide opportunities for meaningful accountability and making amends that do not depend on face-to-face interaction between the victim and offender;
- respect offenders' life experiences, including those with victimisation, and find restorative ways to discuss and address these experiences without absolving responsibility to victims;
- recognise the impact that the prison environment has on prisoners and consider how this experience informs the application of restorative justice in prison; and
- transform the goals and values of prison, not simply add programmes, so that prison can be a place that promotes restorative principles and values.

(Toews, 2002: 6)

A MODEL FOR THE RESTORATIVE PRISON

Belgium establishes restorative prisons

The word 'crisis' means: opportunity; a crucial moment; a turning point; a time of difficulty or distress; an emergency and inevitably a time to decide. How we respond to emergencies reflects the environment in which we find ourselves, the values that prevail in that setting and the courage of leadership to seize the moment.

The response of the Belgian people and their government to the crisis of the Dutroux affair of serial child abuse and child murder in 1996 stands in marked contrast to England's reaction to the murder of two-year-old Jamie Bulger by two young children in Liverpool in 1992. The British established greater control in relation to misbehaviour, became more punitive towards wrong-doers (and particularly the young), and demonised the 'other' within their communities. After the murder and the subsequent press coverage of the trial there was a dramatic rise in the prison population.

When Belgium experienced the horrors of the Dutroux affair their concerns turned towards the institutions of the police and the judiciary and the malfunctioning of the criminal justice system. The decision was made to involve victims in the criminal justice system using the principles of restorative justice — seeking to repair the harm done to victims and communities through the offender so that people could be involved in the process of justice and take responsibility for the outcomes.

The decision to introduce restorative philosophy into prisons was part of this move and has had consequences for all prison systems to consider. The focus was partly in response to the repeatedly formulated requirements of an active self-help group of parents of murdered children and several groups of battered women and partly because there were trends within criminology that gave some direction toward reform. It also reflected the personal courage of politicians to give a lead about what is right rather than follow public opinion.

Victims' demands

From victim surveys, Belgian research showed there was widespread dissatisfaction with the way that public agencies like the police, public prosecutors and judges dealt with the aftermath of crime. Victims expected there to be a public reaction to delinquent behaviour, which included listening to their needs and responding appropriately to their expectations. These goals emphasise the importance of repairing the harm done to individual victims and of the need to restore the confidence of victims, their neighbourhoods and the public belief in the good functioning of the criminal justice system. The Home Office's regular British Crime Surveys show very similar expectations from those most affected by crime.

Trends in criminology

At the same time as awareness of the need to put things right for victims and their communities had increased, there has been much evidence that imprisonment does not deter offenders from future crime. There is also much research that shows that an experience of prison life does not help with the treatment and rehabilitation of the individual offender. In fact the opposite may well be the case — they may be damaged further. This awareness of the failure of custody to change offenders to become safer people and also the demands of victims for personal and community safety prompted a movement into new, alternative ways of operating within the justice system.

Alternative practices

Belgian fieldworkers have collected worldwide examples of successful, new practices in penal procedures. These experiments focused on the restoration of damage caused by crime and on the resolution of conflict between people and within communities. Some examples are:

- a restoration project with juvenile offenders;
- a project about compensation of materials that takes place at the police station;
- the legal possibility of negotiated reaction between offender and public prosecutor; and
- experiments of victim-offender mediation in cases of serious violent crime.

All these experiments were evaluated and all achieved the support of most of the victims, the offenders and the judicial decision-makers. It becomes clear that to be really effective, the victim's perspective must be integrated in all stages of the criminal justice procedure, including any period of custody.

Since 1998, there has been an action research project in six Belgian prisons to test out the possibility of using restorative philosophy within the most controlled social institutions so that prisoners can be enabled to take responsibility for their actions and so that the process can help deal with conflicts between offenders and their victims. The involvement of governors, officers and treatment services was crucial, and the placement of research workers in the prisons contributed to this. The process was evaluated step-by-step to ensure that lessons were regularly learned and good practice identified and spread. Through the results of the initial project, the Minister of Justice decided to introduce restorative activities in all Belgian prisons. Each of the 30 prisons has now appointed a restorative justice consultant. Their role is to work with the governor to introduce restorative justice concepts and practices in line with those developed within the community.

Restorative justice in Belgian prisons

Working towards a restorative custodial policy started in Belgium with the cultivation of a prison culture which allowed and stimulated restoration processes between victims and offenders. In order to begin this change, the whole prison staff were involved in training. Sessions raised awareness amongst staff of restorative theories and practices. Training also took place in basic restorative attitudes to enable staff to discuss the responsibility for the offence and its consequences with the offender without losing his or her confidence. Another attitude developed through this training was multilateral partiality, which involves the therapist to be understanding with the offender and all the other people who are important in his or her living context, such as family, parents, victims and neighbours.

The approach towards prisoners was to help them benefit from a more personal, open way of dealing with the aftermath of crime from the beginning of their period in custody. Staff organized support to help them take up responsibility for the crime and its consequences for victims. This was achieved through individual guidance and group work. Prisoners were given awareness training so they could become conscious of the psychological and emotional consequences their offence caused for victims. This programme is called 'Victim in Focus' and is a confronting approach aimed at changing attitudes.

To prepare victims for this communication-oriented way of solving the problems, better information had to be provided. An information brochure was written to give victims and their neighbours a more realistic view of the situation of imprisoned offenders and what is likely at the end of their sentence. It was important to work with the attitudes of those who supported victims. As long as these supporters stirred up antagonism and polarisation, communication and reparation had no chance.

To help make the community more aware of restorative principles, an informative game was created. In this game, young people learned how to deal with conflicts in a more constructive way.

Restorative activities in practice

To reduce the polarisation between victim aid services and offender aid services, discussion groups between the treatment staff of the prison and those from the victim and offender aid services were organized. These professionals became aware of the problems the others face in achieving their work and built bridges between each other. They also explored the possibilities and the limits for victim-offender communication while the offender is imprisoned.

When victims and offenders requested direct contact, an experienced victim-offender mediator was called upon. The mediator spent much time gradually approaching the matter, understanding each party before the direct meeting. It was also possible to have indirect communication by go-betweens, and this was arranged through the most appropriate methods.

Group sessions were also arranged between prisoners with victims. People who had a victim experience (but not the victims of the prisoners) came to bear witness. These meetings were considered to be vital for the healing process of the victim as well as making the offender more sensitive to the short and long-term consequences of being the victim of an offence.

Once communication was established, it was important to provide possibilities to do something constructively towards the victim. This was through apologies, financial compensation or working on personal problems. Within prison staff and the prisoners themselves, different ways were worked out to express this wish to repair the harm and to do something constructive for the victim or their neighbourhood.

Prisoners had access to a restoration fund which was started to enable them to earn money to pay some restitution towards the victim and to establish some communication. The financial benefit from the fund was achieved through the prisoner carrying out some community work either in the prison or in the community. Any reward they got went to the victim. This gave the offender the possibility to give concrete expression to his or her wish to restore.

In order to change attitudes of people from the local community one project worker organized prison visits and group meetings between outsiders and prisoners. Police, victims and interested people attended these events and experienced the atmosphere of life in prison. Evaluation of these visits established that they were important for the self-esteem of prisoners and prison staff and that they changed the attitude of the visitors towards imprisoned people.

Future possibilities

The research team reported on its preliminary work, describing the difficulty of reconciling the basic values of restorative justice within prison law and administration. Restorative justice requires respect, the assuming of responsibility and the freedom to solve the problems by those involved in the conflict. These attitudes are opposed to the deprivation of freedom and limited personal responsibility that form the basis of current prison practice. The tension between the new policy and past practice is clearly evident and further dynamic growth will be required to reconcile these issues.

The restorative paradigm is very demanding, requiring policies about offenders, about victims and about the restoration between victims and offenders. The challenging concept is that prisoners are fully responsible for their own lives and for their acts. Offenders who are not yet prepared to assume their responsibilities should get opportunities during a prison sentence to work on their basic problems. Thus prisons should provide legal information, mediation, professional training and therapeutic treatment. Victims need an environment of support to get through their bad experience so they can give themselves and the offender new chances to take up their lives in a community of trust.

Restorative justice in Belgian prisons must be seen in the context of a restorative policy in the whole of that criminal justice system. A restorative approach is employed at the police station at arrest, during the investigation period and by the judge and barristers at court. At all stages of the process, victim orientation and the possibilities for mediation, reparation, community service or other alternative ways to react to lawbreaking are becoming the norm.

Visiting three prisons

Box 1: Leuven Central

A radial prison built in the mid-nineteenth century provides a long-term training setting for 300 male prisoners. Its unique regime enables a full day of unlocked movement with access to work, education and association. Men are selected to come to the prison and places are valued because of the relaxed regime and the proximity to home for many prisoners.

The prison was selected for the first phase of the restorative justice project and had a researcher working with staff to examine processes that were already restorative and to review those that could be introduced to help achieve the objectives of developing a culture of respect within the prison and to facilitate direct communication between the prisoners and the victim. The expectation of quick action was unrealistic even after the conclusion of the research phase and the introduction of a consultant to work with the Governor in order to achieve structural change.

The consultant has helped raise staff awareness of the principles of restorative justice and has worked with a group of staff committed to the concepts to implement procedures within the prison for individual prisoners and groups. Thus the concepts were then readily seen in action through the relationships between staff and staff, staff and prisoners, and prisoners and prisoners. The development of the regime has been recognised by the Governor who is aware of the underpinning effect of the concern for victims that prevails in her decision-making about prisoners and in the relationships between her staff, the prisoners and the community.

In implementing restorative justice in Belgian prisons there were several factors that were supportive to the process. These included: the victim movement that had been strong for the past decade and had established through legislation an obligation for the police to inform them about offenders, their trial and the outcome; the government appointment of a coordinator at Crown Prosecution Service level; and an active victim support service. Offenders owe much to their victims and the community through the court process as the costs of the trial are often ordered to be paid by the offender and there is often a civil action that determines the level of compensation to be paid by the offender to the victim. The development of the Restoration Fund that enables prisoners to earn money to pay to their victims provides an important opportunity for them to exercise responsibility in making some reparation.

Box 2: Hoogstraten Penitentiary School Centre

In the remarkable setting of a moated medieval castle, this open prison for 150 medium term prisoners provides a community regime based on a full working day (starting work at seven in the morning) with a range of vocational training to ensure good preparation for realistic release. The prisoners are prepared for a full reintegration into society in the expectation that this will improve community safety. The regime is integrated to support this creative resettlement approach.

Restorative justice ideas are closely congruent with the approach of the regime to seek the development of responsibility in prisoners and their effective return to the community as responsible people. The development of the role of prisoners taking responsibility for the organization of events as auxiliary staff was a marked reflection of this aim.

The development of restorative work at Hoogstraten was influenced by two theories — *healing through meeting*, developed by Martin Buber, and *multi-lateral partiality* (the capacity to have empathy for all sides of a conflict). Developments from these theories have led the staff to consider the need to integrate some of the divisions in society and to develop circles of sympathy for the prison and within the communities to which prisoners return.

The process through which the work has been developed has been through educational workshops, though guided visits to the prison and through direct mediation.

- The workshops for prisoners are to help develop the awareness of the harm they have caused, to develop empathic possibilities and new skills reflecting the respect for cultural differences within the prisoner group. The aim is to help develop communication skills so that prisoners can speak from the heart. Workshops are assisted by the presence of victims who give their testimony. This can lead to a strong sense of empowerment of both sides, as the atmosphere is one of meeting as a person, not as an object or role, but as someone with a story, a family and a history.
- Guided visits are to encourage the introduction of the community into the prison with the hope that they will then become involved in other events in the prison. Staff and prisoners are involved in the process which can be arranged specially for potential employers of prisoners on release.
- Direct mediation between prisoners and victims has started and is at an early stage of development. With dedicated resources to this function and the awareness that the work has to be conducted with great sensitivity there is an increasing demand for this service.

Box 3: Leuven Hulp

A busy, overcrowded support prison to Leuven Central, Hulp contains 165 prisoners, 90 of whom are awaiting trial, with 35 psychiatrically ill prisoners and about 50 locally based men who are held as close to home as possible. The Governor outlined the purpose of the prison as being:

- to hold men in such a way that their social contacts remain intact as far as possible;
- to offer them opportunities for development during their custody; and
- to pay attention to developing the quality of interactions between staff and staff, prisoner and prisoner, and staff and prisoner.

The project in Hulp was one of the pilot ones and the workers involved recognised there was no blueprint with which to approach the task. The work was commenced with consultation with the whole staff through meetings to consider and raise awareness of the direction of the prison, the social and victim support services available locally and the support services for offenders. Through this a working group was set up by the more active staff to develop the ideas further in action.

The preparation and distribution of a leaflet to inform victims about the prison system, parole, release and regimes was an important part of raising awareness. The debts that prisoners have incurred to the state and their victims are burdens upon them that they can alleviate through community work to earn money to pay off these debts. This Restoration Fund, set up through community concern about encouraging prisoners to accept responsibility for the future, enables prisoners to pay something back through their own working efforts.

In Hulp a particular project called 'Focus on Victims' has been established to raise awareness, develop empathy and change attitudes towards victims. This process starts early in the prisoner's experience in custody and groups of about eight men work at the issues for about 30 hours a month with staff and victims coming into the prison. Although there is often some resistance and indifference to victims from prisoners initially, the experience of the course has been that through multi-lateral partiality there has been much growth and sensitivity developed to enable prisoners to behave responsibly towards those they have harmed.

CHAPTER 5

What a Restorative Justice Prison Would Look Like

This chapter will present an image of a fully restorative prison, including:

- a continuum of restorative justice involvement, from a single project to a whole prison commitment;
- examples of how restorative justice could work in induction, race relations and diversity, adjudications, anti-bullying and violence reduction, and preparation for release; and
- specific descriptions of how pre-release, anti-bullying and the handling of complaints work.

THE FOUNDATIONS OF A RESTORATIVE PRISON

Marian Liebmann wrote that the way to develop restorative justice is to think creatively; not get bound up by current obstacles or objections.

> Like an artist with a palette of colours, I will not restrict myself to what is already available, or what is financially feasible. Rather I will use my imagination to paint a picture of how things could be ... What could a system of restorative justice look like?
> (Cited in Quill and Wynne, 1993)

This chapter is intended to dream about how a prison could be if it were guided by a primary commitment to practise restorative justice.

Restorative principles and practice can influence prisons in a range of ways. Six levels can be seen on a continuum. These comprise:

1. individuals conducting conferences or victim-offender mediation as needed with serving prisoners;
2. projects that build on partnerships between a single establishment and an outside organization;
3. projects that work with a number of establishments to facilitate restorative approaches;
4. a package of restorative approaches, developed jointly with prison management in a number of prisons;
5. initiatives owned and driven by prison staff to influence the running of the prison; and
6. a whole prison commitment to incorporate restorative justice into its mission, so that the establishment chooses restorative justice as its paradigm.

The first few levels have been established already; at least they have been piloted in specific prisons. The last two take the ideal of the restorative prison to its logical conclusion, whereby the whole function of imprisonment could be devoted to restorative aims.

1. Individuals conducting conferences or victim-offender mediation as needed with serving prisoners
For some years, there have been restorative projects based in the community that involve prisons. These activities engage victims, community members and prisoners, and aim to acknowledge and try to put right the harm done through crime. Restorative practitioners like Barbara Tudor, who is based in the West Midlands Probation Service, have been mediating between victims of serious offences and prisoners and their families to reach a closer understanding of what happened, who has been affected, with what consequences, and to bring about some healing in their lives.

2. Projects building on partnerships between a single establishment and an outside body
Several projects have developed as partnerships between an agency in the community and the staff of an institution. Central Mediation Services has worked with Brinsford Young Offender Institution near Wolverhampton to raise the awareness of offenders to the experience of victims. The work gained a Butler Trust Award for the member of Brinsford staff primarily involved. Victims of crime in the Sandwell and Dudley area are asked by the Mediation Service if they want to have information about the offender and want to relay any message. Following this, the young man in custody is contacted with the support of prison staff and is asked if he would like to give any information or relay a message to the victim. This process leads to second-hand messages, letters of regret and sometimes meetings between the main parties with a mediator so that the dialogue can take place face to face. The evidence is that this contact helps the victims feel more in control and that the young men feel they have taken more responsibility for their actions. There are some remarkable stories arising from this enterprise and their experience gives hope for the potential of similar work in the future if it were supported by adequate funding and commitment.

The International Centre for Prison Studies and the Inside Out Trust (IOT) worked with HMP Holme House, Kirklevington House and Deerbolt YOI, to transform a run-down Albert Park in Middlesborough. This, the Restorative Prison Project, was an example of enterprising community involvement by which those in custody participated in a process of making amends. Time-limited, clearly defined projects such as these can broaden the views of policy-makers about what is possible. They can have a profound effect on organizations by providing new stories of effective practices.

3. Projects that work with a number of establishments to facilitate restorative approaches
An exciting research project now taking place in the Thames Valley offers adult offenders in prison for serious violent offences an opportunity for a conference with their victims and their communities of care. So far, there have been over 50 conferences in HMP Bullingdon, Oxfordshire. The conferences—and the involvement of prison officers, probation officers and community mediators in facilitating them—have had a considerable impact on the life of the prison and

on the attitude of prisoners to restorative work. The project provides a rare opportunity for prisoners and victims of serious crime to engage in dialogue. Prison staff and managers have gained an appreciation of the potential of the process.

A similar effort is the Sycamore Tree Project, which is a faith-based approach, working in many prisons to support offenders in acknowledging the harm caused through their crimes.

4. A package of restorative approaches, developed jointly with prison management in a number of prisons

The Restorative Justice in Prisons Project, carried out in 2001-2, introduced restorative principles into the operations of three prisons: Bristol, Norwich and Winchester (Thames Valley Partnership, 2002). Specific examples of this work are described below. This project piloted the ideas behind circles and restorative conferencing to conflict resolution in custodial settings in England. Part of this project has explored the procedures for consultation and communication among staff and between staff and prisoners.

Inside Out Trust operates workshops in many prisons in England and Wales. Prisoners are provided with opportunities to make amends, in a general way, by repairing goods such as bicycles or eyeglasses. The finished articles are then distributed to charitable causes. IOT also trains prisoners in transcribing books into Braille and then distributes their work. Prisoners view themselves in a different light as they see the value of their contribution, and the outside community may come to a new understanding of the humanity of offenders. Their work in prisons is currently being evaluated.

5. Initiatives owned and driven by prison staff to influence the running of the prison

Evidence from the Restorative Justice in Prisons Project shows that the process of introducing restorative work can bring about a conceptual change in staff practices. Building from a piecemeal use of restorative justice as an 'add-on', the prison adopted a restorative ethos as its preferred method in a range of areas, for example, the way that staff concerns were managed. Staff grievance procedures, personnel management practice and the resolution of complaints from prisoners and public were all re-considered from a restorative perspective.

6. A whole prison commitment to incorporate restorative justice into its mission, so that the establishment chooses restorative justice as its paradigm

A whole prison commitment to restorative approaches would re-define prisons as places of reform and resettlement. Prisons now have an opportunity to become places for creating change in individuals and society rather than for administering punishment. A whole prison approach will lead to strategies for applying restorative principles of inclusion, flexibility and problem-solving. The experience of therapeutic communities such as HMP Grendon is particularly relevant in this respect. In therapeutic community prisons, there is an expectation that all prisoners and all staff will be accountable for their actions and decisions, contributing to building a caring community.

The last area encompasses the organizational structure above establishment level. National prison policy could be transformed by restorative justice to prioritise healing and personal responsibility. Restorative models seem to be in stark conflict with the move towards top-down centrally controlled management systems, which Government demands from public sector agencies. Restorative approaches are strong in providing accountability within their own circles. In theory, the Government supports restorative justice, but it is not clear if Government is willing to change its response to crime from a focus on law-breaking to a concern for the harm done. Nor is it clear that the Government is committed to promoting genuine empowerment and inclusiveness. It is possible that statutory agencies might be slower to appreciate restorative justice than the public, particularly if the former are preoccupied with targets and a modernising agenda.

OPERATIONAL APPLICATIONS OF RESTORATIVE JUSTICE

Reflecting on the Restorative Justice in Prisons Project, it is possible to see opportunities for restorative processes across the full range of functional activities in prisons. The following are offered as possible examples (the actual use in any prison depends on how the staff apply restorative justice to meet their specific needs).

Induction programmes for prisoners At the very beginning of a sentence, prisoners are often at their most receptive to new ideas. At this time, the example set by other prisoners can show how it is possible to take responsibility for the harm done and to start to make amends. Induction programmes can encourage this process by demonstrating values of respect for all prisoners, irrespective of the nature of their offences, an open ear to their expression of need, and inclusiveness, welcoming them as members of the prison community.

Sentence management and planning Prisoners will be involved as primary stakeholders in the development of sentence plans. From the restorative justice perspective, it is vital that these plans hold prisoners to account for their behaviour. Sentence plans will focus on empowering offenders to consider the effects of their behaviour on their victims. This approach also helps staff to see the offence within the wider context of the community and the victim's needs. (See also *Chapter 6*, on the SEU Report).

Equality, diversity and race relations Race relations are unusually well-suited to restorative justice. A commitment to a non-blaming approach, guiding a conference or mediation, can bring to the surface different perspectives that shape racial incidents. A typical prison investigation into racial allegations employs an adversarial approach, the effect of which is to inhibit open dialogue.

Complaints and requests More broadly, restorative justice suggests that any complaint be dealt with in a person-to-person format, where each person should be expected to explain their thinking (see below).

Adjudications The disciplinary hearing, a key function in the enforcement of rules, sets the tone for staff attitudes and prisoner compliance. Restorative justice can introduce a dramatically different way of strengthening social order (see above, *Chapter 3*).

Anti-bullying strategy Restorative approaches counter the power imbalances that drive bullying, providing support for the victim, identifying the exploitation as unfair and hurtful, and drawing the offender to a commitment not to continue (see below).

Anti-violence strategy From the perspective of conventional prison discipline, violence is against the rules and is caused by disruptive and dangerous individuals. Through restorative justice, assaults and fights can be understood as the end results of conflicts or disputes between prisoners. The strategy for reducing violence begins by training staff and prisoners in conflict awareness and mediation skills, perhaps through a programme like the AVP (Alternatives to Violence Project) or through NVC (Non-Violent Communication). Establishing peer mediators, as with the 'Listeners' programme for suicide prevention, will play to the strengths of many prisoners in managing difficult settings and in being able to support each other.

Offending behaviour courses Victim empathy and accountability for criminal behaviour are expressed in these programmes in which prisoners take responsibility for their behaviour. This is an ideal setting in which to express contrition and compliance with a reparative scheme. Accredited courses could be strengthened by restorative approaches as they are then placed in a wider and more legitimate context.

Prison outreach Staff and prisoners can serve the community by educating groups about the effect of imprisonment through sharing information about prisons and life stories of offenders. This can be very effective when done in an understanding and positive way which is not designed to scare.

Staffing processes In order to integrate restorative practices, principles and processes into the life of a prison, it is important that staff feel that they are treated with respect and consideration. Mediation and conferencing, facilitated by trained restorative justice practitioners, can be offered to staff for dealing with their disputes and conflicts. The management of staff should operate with the same principles of concern for the individual and respect for their personal development within the professional setting.

Preparation for release When prisoners are full partners in sentence planning, many restorative justice possibilities arise for them to accept responsibility for their crimes, establish accountability for the future to victims, primary and secondary, and commit themselves to the community to which they will return. The resources of the prison—work, education, leisure, offending behaviour courses and other programmes—can be channelled to this effect.

Resettlement Preparation for reintegration should start at the beginning of a sentence and should engage the agencies that are likely to be affected by the prisoner's release, such as housing, health and employment, as well as the criminal justice agencies of police and probation. A conference with family and community agencies while the prisoner is on home leave or temporary release from prison, with the prison providing some feedback about the course of the sentence and about future expectations, should make the process more purposeful. Family and victims should be involved in this process (if willing).

Circles on release Once released, prisoners can often experience difficulties in sustaining the plans and the good intentions they formed when in custody. Sometimes, there is a need for community support. A good example of how this can be provided is the Circles of Support and Accountability Project, which has been developed for high risk, high need sex offenders. Members of the community volunteer to provide support and to hold offenders accountable through regular involvement, weekly meetings and presence through difficult times. Volunteers working with justice agencies have added a new dimension of safety and risk management for a sensitive group of offenders seeking to become part of the community again.

PRE-RELEASE, ANTI-BULLYING AND COMPLAINTS

Let us imagine, in further detail, how a restorative prison would work, using as examples three key functions: pre-release, anti-bullying and complaints. These have been selected from the list of functions above to show how restorative justice could be practised in the day-to-day life of a prison.

Pre-release
Resettlement, the return to the community after a prison sentence, is often perceived as risky by prisoners and as unwelcome by their wider community. Restorative approaches give the offender and the community opportunities to try creative solutions to problems of reintegration and reconciliation.

A restorative process draws on the energy and input of the offender's family, her victim(s), the community to which she will return, the criminal justice system, and other agencies that will continue to be involved with her. Restorative justice promotes relationships of mutual accountability as it honours the equal status of all who have a stake in the offender's future.

A conference at the pre-release stage explores the dynamic relationships between prisoner and community. The key stakeholders involved in the process of receiving her back into the community are invited. Such a conference provides all with an opportunity to review together such issues about the return home as:

- any unresolved anxieties remaining from the offence;
- the risks that community members feel are still present;
- any public commitment the prisoner may wish to make to the agencies and community members;
- the concern the family may have about their involvement by association with her;
- the responsibilities any agencies may have to maintain supervision and vigilance.

The conference is convened by an independent community-based agency, because their neutral involvement will provide focus and legitimacy for the process of sharing concerns and reaching understandings. The facilitators prepare for the meeting by outlining:

- the purpose of the meeting, namely, to provide a safe and inclusive forum to prepare for the prisoner to leave prison, to benefit the prisoner, her family and the community;
- the process, an arranged meeting of interested stakeholders to discuss concerns and seek resolutions, gain understanding and develop an agreement for future action from all parties;
- the desired outcome, which is that everyone will have been able to voice their concerns and face each other rather than harbour anxieties, resentments, suspicions and fears.

During the conference, the prison plays an important role in supporting the prisoner. In part this requires the prison to describe the process, gains and problems inherent in a prison sentence—particularly as the sentence comes to its conclusion. A probation officer may be best placed to support the family during the conference in relation to the pain they have experienced during the sentence, or to voice their ongoing concerns of adjusting back with the family changed. The police may wish to represent the concerns of the community or to be there in support of the victim. They may also be willing to make a commitment to support the offender in relation to risk of relapse.

Thus the conference addresses points of tension, enabling both the prisoner and the community to prepare for the release. Restorative justice's open approach enables the prisoner to communicate her progress, her concerns about returning to the community and her intentions on release. It also identifies key agencies, individuals and groups who could assist in the process of return (as a 'community of care').

The meeting concludes with a written agreement in which the prisoner makes certain explicit commitments (including, for example, ongoing treatment programmes). Community groups offer support and involvement. The agencies outline their responsibilities and define expectations of support available. And the family accept the complexity of the situation within which they may be able to support their loved one.

Follow-up to the resettlement conference is achieved through subsequent home leaves and in-prison work—and eventually on the prisoner's release through supervision.

Other examples of restorative justice make clear that a major benefit for victims and offenders is the reassurance that they feel when they have had a say in the process. This sense of ownership is reflected in the higher completion rate of action plans subsequent to a restorative justice conference than in other non-custodial disposals. The likelihood of the process assisting in resettlement is considerable and any project commenced should evaluate the effectiveness of the approach both in relation to reconviction rates and also in terms of the prisoner's feelings about returning from prison and those of the community receiving the prisoner back.

Using this model of restorative justice:

- the complexity of the process of the offender returning to her community is evident;

- the need for the key agencies — police, prisons, probation — to work together becomes clear; and
- the need to pay regard to the offender's community (family), the victim and her family and the community groups in the locality is also apparent.

Anti-bullying

How would an emphasis on harm and on resolving conflicts change how prisons respond to bullying?

Bullying has been defined as a relationship in which a person establishes dominance over someone through intimidation and exploits that dominance persistently. Ironically, bullying is not an infringement of prison rules. However, many prisons maintain a zero tolerance policy regarding bullying. Most prison-based anti-bullying programmes entail a series of steps, beginning with the identification of a suspected bully; a warning combined with surveillance of the suspect; and then a programme to tackle the bully's behaviour, such as segregation from the wing, attempts to change attitudes and reduced privileges.

How do prisons expect staff to identify bullies? *Figures 1* and *2* show methods used in two prisons, based on a list of behaviours that are believed to indicate bullying.

HMP ********* Anti-bullying form

Bullying monitoring. Has the inmate displayed any of the following towards staff or inmates:

Verbal abuse

Long direct eye contact

Nose to nose confrontation

Shouting at people

Physical abuse (i.e., punching, pushing, play fighting)

Threatening gestures, pointing, aggressive body gestures

Persistent demands of staff

Behaviour around the hot plate — demanding extra food, etc.

Does he/she try to get extra time on the phone?

Does he/she try to borrow other inmates' possessions, e.g. phone cards?

Has he/she been found in possession of items that do not belong to him/her?

Is he/she operating a 2 for 1 business, i.e., taxing, theft from cells?

Any other anti-social behaviour?

Has he/she been placed on a Governor's report?

Figure 1: Anti-bullying form

HMP ******** *Anti-Bullying statement*

Do you ...

➢ Put pressure on other prisoners who are weaker than you?
➢ Force others to join in drug taking or other illicit activities and
  make them feel weak if they don't?
➢ Persuade other prisoners to smuggle contraband through visits
  or bring it back from temporary release?
➢ Think it's okay to intimidate or assault sex offenders?
➢ Think it's okay to intimidate or assault other prisoners who have
  been labelled as 'Grasses'?
➢ Get other prisoners into debt and then threaten them when they
  can't pay up?

If you do any of these things, then

you are a bully.

Figure 2: Prison warning to bullies

Listing behaviour that indicates bullying is flawed in a number of ways. First, no list can be exhaustive. Prisoners can persistently dominate and exploit other prisoners without engaging in any of the behaviours listed in an anti-bullying statement; or can engage in any of them without bullying.

Second, as a list of behaviours cannot define bullying precisely, prisoners will not be able to know in advance what kind of actions are allowed and which will result in their being labelled a bully. Knowing in advance the boundaries of accepted behaviour is a basic requirement of natural justice. Anti-bullying programmes can lead to the arbitrary targeting of individual prisoners.

Finally, prisoners in conflicts almost always engage in mutual harm. It is very difficult for anyone external to their conflict to judge whether one person had power over the other, or whether the foes had equal power (and were not, by definition, bullying). Anti-bullying work is changing, but the following description is typical of many establishments.

When an officer identifies a prisoner being bullied, the officer takes control of the situation in order to protect him or her from further harm. The victim is very rarely asked what he or she would like to happen. The victim might be moved off the wing for their protection; or remain on the wing while officers remove the suspected bully. But it is unlikely that the victim will be given a genuine opportunity to influence how the situation is handled. The staff thereby deny the victim any chance of assuming an adult, responsible role with regard to his or her own reaction to the bullying behaviour.

Victims are likely to react to this treatment by feeling still more powerless. In addition, other prisoners might draw the conclusion that the victim needs to depend on staff to protect them, and this may mark them out as weak and vulnerable to exploitation. Worse, prisoners might suspect that the person who was bullied informed on the bully, and this perceived betrayal will mark them out for more isolation and scorn.

Following guidance about what to look for (the lists of bullying behaviours are typical) the first step for staff in enforcing discipline is to identify the bully. The second step usually involves a warning, confronting the prisoner with an ultimatum to change or be placed on an anti-bullying programme. Many anti-bullying programmes use threats to coerce prisoners into less domineering behaviour. The way they treat prisoners models the use of superior power to force someone into compliance, reinforcing the message that coercion and intimidation are legitimate.

When threatened with punishment, these prisoners are likely to react defensively, perhaps by arguing that the victims' behaviour merited such aggression or by under-stating the harm done. They will not argue that bullying is a good thing; they are much more likely to claim that what they were doing was not bullying. Because it is a stigmatising label, they are also likely to deny that they are a bully.

Prisoners whom staff define as bullies are then isolated (often being moved off the wing to a special unit). Separating them from their peers and defining them publicly as a bully can undermine any chance of a change in their behaviour. The prisoner will feel resentful at being picked out and punished for behaviour that is far more widespread. There is also a risk that labelling them a bully may increase the stature they have among their peers.

In some ways, the traditional response to bullying relationships compounds the problem with methods that confirm the weakness of the victim and uphold the principle that differences are settled by superior force. Anti-bullying policies share an insight that the defining characteristic of bullying is power. Bullying occurs when one person has established and exploited power over another. But if bullying is an abuse of power, then what are the best methods to use to remedy the situation? How does restorative justice change the way that prisons would treat victims of bullying?

First, restorative approaches achieve empowerment: victims value the chance to give their input in reaching an agreement about how to resolve the problem. People do not want to be stuck in the role of a victim of bullying; they grasp opportunities to regain control of their lives. In the prison context, victims might feel they have few options other than to assault the person who was intimidating them. Hitting out, they reason, is the best way they can demonstrate to other prisoners that they are not weak, are not targets for further victimisation.

A restorative conference provides a better alternative. Being listened to and having their perspective validated by the conference can be the first step the victim needs to gain self-confidence. The prison does not decide what the victim needs; rather, the victim has the chance to express what *they* would like to happen. In addition, the conference demonstrates that the person who was harmed has a wider community of support. This is crucial because being able to turn to others is one of the most effective ways of countering bullying (which thrives on isolating people from others).

Restorative approaches focus on the harm done. The distinctive perspective that restorative justice brings to bullying suggests a new understanding of the links and differences between harmful behaviour and bullying:

- all bullying is harmful, but not all harmful behaviour is bullying;
- bullying is harm committed within a relationship in which there is a power imbalance. Bullying cannot be mutual. Harmful behaviour does not imply a power difference and can be mutual;
- abusive power is established through the targeted use of harmful behaviour. Harm is the 'toolkit' by which bullying is achieved, maintained and exploited; and
- harmful behaviour is disruptive to social order and reduces safety, whether it is used in a bullying relationship or not.

Brenda Morrison has studied restorative responses to school bullying. She drew up five principles to guide the process of responding to bullying in schools:

1. bullying and being bullied are ways of behaving that can be changed ...
2. addressing wrongdoing, such as bullying, concerns actions and should not involve the denigration of the whole person ...
3. the harm done by bullying to self and others must be acknowledged ...
4. reparation for the harm done is essential ...
5. both bullies and victims are valued members of the school community whose supportive ties with others should be strengthened through participation in communities of care.

(Morrison, 2002: 4)

The aspects of a conference that are likely to steer a suspected bully towards less exploitative behaviour in the future have to do with the emotional process that well-run conferences follow. Morrison's account of a restorative justice response to bullying contrasts with the stigmatising and punitive approach that can sometimes occur in prisons. Three separate points arise from her principles, which we need to discuss in turn: one is focusing on the harm done; two is treating the person who caused the harm with dignity; and three is how restorative justice can level the power disparity between the two prisoners.

Focus on harm
The power of restorative justice to focus on harm rather than guilt brings perpetrators face to face with the emotional damage they have caused. Threats and exploitation are wrong, regardless of who engages in the behaviour.

However, a focus on harm is not sufficient in dealing with all cases of bullying, because many perpetrators will deny or try to minimise the harm done. If perpetrators are told off by a governor or anyone in authority over them and lectured on the harm they have inflicted, the message is likely to be interpreted by the perpetrator as manipulative.

Hence, restorative justice gives priority to direct face-to-face meetings. It is when they must face the person they harmed that the reality of that responsibility comes home to them. Direct contact makes it far more difficult for the perpetrator to deny. But, equally important, the perpetrator is surrounded by his own supporters. A crucial element of the conference is that the perpetrator's behaviour is shameful to those who mean the most to him.

Respect for the dignity of the person who caused harm

Morrison's second principle—focussing on harmful behaviour rather than stigmatising a person—leads to a particular way of responding to bullying and victimisation. The wrongdoer is treated with respect, listened to, and supported; and the emphasis is on reintegrating the wrongdoer.

The typical prison anti-bullying programme confronts the inmate with evidence of their dominating behaviour and puts pressure on them to acknowledge that *they are a bully*, in short, subjecting them to stigma.

In principle, a restorative process supports the person while it condemns his or her actions. The aim of the restorative process is to encourage the person to agree that dominating and exploiting someone else is unacceptable. That way, the bully is in a position freely to decide not to continue exploiting others. Restorative justice can get the prisoner on side, because it maintains a clear distinction between their behaviour and their status as a person. The approach co-opts the person as an equal partner in the process of making good the damage done by the harmful behaviour. This means that far from condemning the perpetrator, the conference leads the person to agree that the harm they caused is wrong. If they accept that, they may be willing to try to make amends.

Morrison wrote:

> The process of shaming requires a confrontation over the wrongdoing between the victim and offender within this community of support. The process is restorative in that the intervention:
>
> - makes it clear to the offender that the behaviour is not condoned within the community; and
> - is supportive and respectful of the individual while not condoning the behaviour.
>
> (Morrison, 2002: 3)

Reversing disparities of power

The change in ethos has the greatest potential in responding to the kind of harmful behaviour—the domination and exploitation—that is central to bullying. Advocates of restorative justice—most notably Heather Strang—have drawn attention to the ability of restorative conferences to even out power disparities. This is a key attribute for a programme intended to reduce bullying.

The structure of a conference gives each person an equal chance to speak uninterrupted. The atmosphere of safety, openness and problem-solving is extremely helpful in empowering the weak and bringing the powerful down to human size. In some ways, conferences with a good number of supporters on both sides are better suited to promoting equal power than small scale, one-to-one mediation.

Morrison confronts the view that the best way to reduce bullying is for staff to remain in full control at all times and that they assert their control through punishment. Restorative approaches actively promote equality of status and power, so that those with a direct stake in the outcome of a dispute have the right to decide, with the support of the school community, what should be done to resolve the conflicts and make amends for the harms done.

A conference brings together two (or more) opposing parties, giving each an equal opportunity to present their view about a problem, in front of supporters of each, representatives of the community, and one (or sometimes two) facilitators. Outside the conference, one participant is much more powerful than the other. But inside the conference, this power advantage is ineffective.

Each side has an equal say — no single party is able to dominate proceedings. Each side has supporters present who are able to challenge any attempt by one or the other party to orchestrate an agreement that suits their purposes to the detriment of the other party. Finally, the face-to-face process encourages each person to see that reaching an agreement is not about power: it is an exercise in cooperation to solve specific problems.

Bullying is a relationship in which one person exercises their power over another. There can be no guarantee that the presence of a neutral facilitator will prevent the dominant person from trying to influence the weaker one in the conference. A subtle signal between the two could be enough to enable the bully to suggest to the victim, 'Whatever happens here, I will get you later.' The potential for the stronger person to try to maintain power through the conference leads to three possible principles for the use of restorative justice in these situations:

- careful preparation by the facilitator(s) prior to the conference is essential and must include the possibility that the facilitator(s) will decide that one or the other is not yet ready for restorative justice;
- in the conference, facilitators need to be vigilant in maintaining the principles of restorative justice, so that all parties know they are respected; and so that victims will be empowered and perpetrators will not feel defensive; and
- the victim's community of care will play a crucial role, staying alert to any evidence of a desire by the perpetrator to hold onto his/her power advantage.

Morrison concluded:

> Restorative justice is about building communities of care around individuals while not condoning harmful behaviour; in other words, holding individuals accountable for their actions within systems of support.
>
> (Morrison, 2002: 2)

Complaints

In order to think about the handling of complaints according to restorative justice, we recall from *Chapter 1* the basic questions restorative justice processes bring to harmful events:

- Describe in your own words what happened.
- What were you thinking at the time?
- Whom do you think has been affected by what happened?
- In what ways were they affected?
- What should happen to put things right?

The restorative justice methods of conferencing or mediation encourage open communication in order to establish what happened, who was affected, in what way and what should be done to put things right. A restorative complaints system contrasts to some current practice, with its secretive process and outcomes that are unsatisfactory for all parties.

The conventional response to a complaint against an officer by a prisoner reinforces the power of management and puts both officer and prisoner in a losing position. Officers have reason to fear that unless they can disprove the evidence for the complaint, their jobs are at risk. Prisoners are dubious of the neutrality in the investigation and the subsequent decision, since complaints are normally investigated by Prison Service employees. Further, the prisoners know that after a complaint is answered, they must return to the wing where the officer (or their colleagues) still possesses considerable informal powers over the prisoner's quality of life.

The conventional handling of complaints is legalistic. It presupposes that the basis of any complaint boils down to a question of fact: either the officer did (or failed to do) what has been claimed, or not. It holds the officer accountable to the system of rules which govern the officers' duties. If the officer acted within the rules, then the complaint is ruled to be groundless, even if the prisoner was treated with palpable disrespect.

The complaints system is also adversarial. It pits all officers against all prisoners, because complaints are only dealt with if they are officially raised by prisoners. Therefore, officers work in the knowledge that any prisoner holds the potential to make an allegation that could put their job at risk. Even if the prisoner has no interest in having an officer punished, the structure means that to complain about treatment sets in motion a process which will either exonerate the officer (suggesting that the prisoner lied) or find the officer guilty (indirectly involving the prisoner in the punitive consequences for the officer).

There are other flaws to the conventional approach, based as it is on investigation of the facts and discipline of the officer. The method assumes that if an officer treated a prisoner unfairly, the officer was fully aware of what he or she was doing. After all, it would be unfair to punish someone for consequences that could not be foreseen. Yet, in practice, this means that the officer is assumed to know in advance how the prisoner will interpret the officer's decision. It is also a weakness that, when an officer was acting in a way that was unfair to the prisoner, the only recourse open to management is to discipline the officer.

Case study

Let us consider a kind of situation that might lead to a complaint, and then picture how a restorative approach might respond. It concerns the way 'Officer Reece' responded to an assault on a black prisoner we will call 'Kevin'[1].

The prisoners are out on exercise. Officer Reece and a colleague are supervising. At the far end of the yard, two white prisoners, 'Ashley' and 'Joe', run up to Kevin and grab him. Joe punches Kevin as Ashley holds him round the waist. Kevin struggles to break free, swinging his arms. At this point, Officer Reece hears the commotion and sees what is happening. From his perspective, he sees Joe and Kevin having a fight and Ashley trying to restrain Kevin. He shouts for them to stop. Kevin is by now badly cut on the face. Officer Reece charges Kevin and Joe with fighting.

At the adjudication, Kevin argues that he was not fighting; he was trying to get away. The Governor hears Officer Reece's evidence and finds Kevin guilty. When Kevin and Joe learn that they were punished equally, Kevin is indignant. Joe agrees to help him. Kevin puts in a complaint against Officer Reece on the grounds that the officer failed to charge one of his assailants, Ashley, with fighting.

At this point, the complaint could be handled as a matter for discipline of staff or through a restorative meeting.

If it were taken up in an investigation, it would lead to one of two outcomes. The Governor could cite the evidence that Kevin was seen by a member of staff swinging his arms about; the evidence was accurate and therefore he was guilty as charged. Case dismissed.

The second possible outcome would be that the Governor accepts the evidence from Joe, that he and Ashley had attacked Kevin. Therefore, the Governor finds that Officer Reece was partial in laying a charge against him. The complaint is upheld and Officer Reece receives a formal warning.

Neither of these outcomes is satisfactory, especially given what we know about the circumstances that led to the complaint. The first outcome would convince a fair-minded prisoner that prison justice is biased and corrupt, and that prisoners will always be treated unfairly. It would also imply that the prison considered Kevin a liar. The second outcome implies that Officer Reece is dishonest or incompetent. But Officer Reece sincerely tried to apply the rules fairly. So, let's look at what might happen if the complaint was handled through mediation.

A trained community mediator, Sue, is asked into the prison to facilitate the process. (Kevin and Officer Reece are reassured that the process will be conducted impartially.)

Sue meets Kevin and hears his story. She also speaks to Joe and Ashley. She hears Officer Reece's version of events. At each point, she informs Kevin and Officer Reece what mediation involves, how it will work, and assures them that it will proceed only if they are willing to continue—the choice is with them. Officer Reece agrees to a mediation, on condition that the mediation involve

---

[1]   The importance of prisons developing mediation as a response to racial complaints is advocated in a Home Office study by Kimmett Edgar and Carol Martin (2004).

Kevin, Sue, a governor—and no one else. Sue consults Kevin, who agrees with the arrangements.

Sue begins the meeting by pointing out that she is not there to take sides. In this particular form of mediation, she will be practising a no-blame approach. She will ask both people to tell their stories, but she will also ask the other person to listen, not to interrupt and to try to appreciate the other person's perspective.

Sue says that she could start with either person, and then asks Officer Reece to relate what he recalled of the incident. Mr Reece says that he was on duty at exercise and heard a noise. He saw Kevin swinging his arms at Joe, and he saw Ashley trying to restrain Kevin. Although he could see that Kevin was injured, it was his duty (he explains) to charge both with fighting since he directly witnessed Kevin swinging at Joe.

Sue asks Officer Reece if he considered that it was possible that Kevin was acting in self-defence. Officer Reece agrees that that was possible, but he explains that in his understanding of the rules, throwing punches at another prisoner counts as fighting and to be fair, both must be charged. He adds that it is not his job to decide who is to blame: he presents his evidence and the Governor makes the decision.

Sue asks Kevin for his story. He explains that he was minding his own business on exercise when two prisoners came up and attacked him. He denies that he struck Joe, and says that he is still very angry about being charged with fighting. Being accused of fighting was, he says, as hurtful as the fact that he was attacked.

Sue asks Kevin whether he felt it was possible that when the officer saw the incident it might appear that he and Joe were fighting and Ashley was trying to stop the fight. He replies, with some impatience, that it is the officers' job to see what is happening and not to make snap judgments. He repeats that he did not punch Joe and says that he would like to call him in to support him.

Sue reminds him that this is not an adjudication and they are not there to dispute the other person's experience. She says that the meeting was called because he felt that he had been treated unfairly by Officer Reece and both of them wanted to clear the air.

The Governor asks Sue if she can make a comment. The Governor says that she now sees how this situation developed. She understands that officers cannot always know what a prisoner's intentions are. Even though it appeared that Ashley was trying to stop the fight, it was possible (the Governor says) that he was actually an accomplice to an assault.

Officer Reece raises his hand. He speaks directly to Kevin. He says, 'I want you to know I think you are a very helpful and cooperative person and an asset to the wing. I do not hold any ill-feeling toward you and I can now understand your point of view about this incident. I did what I thought was fair, but if what you say is true, then I should have charged Ashley, too.'

Kevin's anger begins to fade. He speaks directly to Officer Reece, 'I guess it would be asking too much to say I won't really be satisfied until you withdraw the charge of fighting. I got on okay with you in the past and I would like to think we can keep a good relationship in future. But I still think this matter was dealt with unfairly.'

The Governor says something about the possibility of re-opening the adjudication. But then Sue explains that though that would be welcomed, it is not really the purpose of the meeting. The mediation was called because there was a conflict between Officer Reece and Kevin. To work, the meeting would need to make clear what Officer Reece and what Kevin wanted to happen, and then see if they — not the Governor — can propose a solution.

Kevin makes the first move, stating that he is willing to accept it was an honest mistake and he holds out his hand to Mr Reece. Mr Reece shakes his hand and then says that he was sorry that Kevin was hurt. Mr Reece adds that he will be more careful in the future not to jump to conclusions. The facilitator concludes the meeting, stating that she will write up the agreement for both to sign.

This was a hypothetical complaints mediation, based on a real case. In *Appendix I* we have included an actual mediation. Together, the two show some of the ways that mediation can provide a more sensitive way of dealing with complaints against staff, one in which enmity is reduced and constructive solutions become possible. Mediation is attractive to many because of its open approach to people's feelings, its clear neutrality, and its equal respect for all parties. Direct meetings, facilitated by a trained mediator, have an amazing power to work through anger and defensiveness, and to increase mutual understanding.

CONCLUSION

In this chapter, we have begun the process of sketching how mainstream prison processes can be transformed if they are guided by restorative principles. To explore these possibilities, expanding the repertoire of restorative approaches and applying its principles to a wider range of situations, prison staff need to think creatively about how problems might be addressed by applying restorative values. For example, how can staff:

- focus on the harm that needs to be healed;
- practise respect, trust and voluntarism;
- empower prisoners, and form an emotionally safe setting with confidentiality and open listening; and
- promote mutual personal accountability and inclusive problem-solving techniques?

How can they bring these values to life, in the day-to-day duties of prison officers and managers, such as reception and induction, sentence planning, kit change, canteen provision, prison jobs, Incentives and Earned Privileges, drugs strategy and diversity?

The stories in this chapter are intended to encourage prison staff to take on restorative values and methods and work with experienced practitioners from the community to find ways to apply the approach to everyday problems in the prison. Although it is not in the style of restorative justice to be prescriptive about the steps one must take to develop the concept, the examples used do provide a sense of direction. In that sense, this book is a work in progress, as it leaves to the reader the task of working out how to apply restorative justice more broadly than at present. By looking at some key areas — pre-release, anti-bullying and complaints — we have indicated how restorative justice would transform the conventional approach. These examples suggest ways that restorative justice can make these processes much more sensitive to the needs of victims, offenders and prison staff.

CHAPTER 6

The Restorative Sentence

RESPONSIBILITY IN SENTENCING

How can I make the best use of the sentence? That is the key question that every person sentenced by a court could be encouraged to ask—and the question that those responsible for managing the sentence, if it involves supervision or custody, could be asking so that those sentenced might take responsibility for their sentence.

This would undoubtedly help focus the sentence towards a restorative culture in that accepting responsibility for the sentence and the offence for which it was incurred will inevitably lead the offender to think about the impact of the offence upon the victim and their community; and on the offender's community as well.

Sentencers, at whatever level and of whatever offender age group, should be asking what they might do to encourage responsible participation in sentencing (including the whole experience as being within the concern of the court). That can be as simple as asking the defendant and HM Prison Service to inform the court about what work might be undertaken over the course of the sentence.

The Sentencing Guidelines Council (SGC) has a superb opportunity to include these twin propositions which underlie responsible sentencing in the SGC's own principles. All sentences might reasonably be expected to serve a reparative aim. Offenders should all be examined to see what they might offer towards that aim.

It would be of great help to people working with restorative justice in the criminal justice system to know that prisoner and prison had been enjoined to work restoratively from the outset.

While the public has a right to expect sentences to protect them and make the community safer, political leaders should make clear that there are limits to the extent to which sentences can be highly retributive without actually wasting public money. It would help to have a clear strategy which puts offender responsibility and the courts' support for it at the centre of sentencing.

THE RESPONSIBLE SENTENCE

What would a responsible sentencing framework mean? The strategy would have five main elements:

1. Offenders should be required to answer for their offences by cooperating with a responsible sentence plan;

2. The courts should make clear that such responsibility will be recognised in the sentence, and agencies will be held accountable for sentence plan commitments;

3. Victims should be given all relevant information about these elements in order to decide what if any view they wish the sentencer to note;

4. Resources identified as necessary to honour responsible sentence plans should take priority in allocating budgets; and

5. Purely retributive proportions of sentences should be identified as such, and their contribution to the overall sentence should be strictly limited to a small part of the total with reasons given for believing that this element is proportional to the gravity of the offence and the guilt of the offender.

Responsible sentencing offers an invitation to take and give responsibility as a basis for preserving and promoting responsible behaviour. We should be particularly careful to do this in sentencing, if we want to live in a more peaceful and productive society, because of the implications of excluding people. We should test all of our criminal justice processes and assumptions against the needs of responsible sentencing. The sentencers should be included as the primary commissioners of prison sentences in order to reverse the courts' unaccountable over-use of custody, which has become so routine.

There is general agreement among practitioners and academics that the criminal justice system will not succeed in its aim of reducing re-offending, or even in providing a stable framework for penal custody and supervision, unless there is a reasonable alignment between the demands which the courts' sentencing practice — including that stemming from SGC guidance — makes on the Prison Service and its capacity to give effect to the sentences that courts impose. That capacity includes accommodation and other physical resources, programmes, facilities and skills on a sufficient scale and of suitable quality to reduce offending behaviour.

The need for that alignment has been regularly expressed over the last 30 years, and at various times before that, but always from the point of view of the Prison Service and Probation Service as providers. The argument has rarely, if ever, been put forward from the point of view of the courts — that courts must take account of the system's capacity if they are to achieve their own purposes in sentencing. That argument was not important when the purposes of sentencing were not defined but courts saw them principally as retribution and deterrence, with rehabilitation as an optional extra for others, such as probation officers, prison staff and volunteers, to achieve if they were able to do so.

The Criminal Justice Act 2003 transforms the situation via its introduction of five statutory purposes of sentencing — purposes which the courts as well as the operational services now have a statutory responsibility to seek to achieve:

- punishment of offenders;
- reduction of crime (including its reduction by deterrence);
- reform and rehabilitation of offenders;
- protection of the public; and
- making of reparation by offenders to people affected by their offences.

To achieve an alignment between sentencing practice and the Prison Service's capacity requires:

- the courts to acknowledge that they themselves have a responsibility to sentence in a way which will enable the purposes of sentencing to be achieved;
- prisons and probation services to maximise their resources within the budget available, and to deploy them to the best possible effect in accordance with those purposes; and
- a relationship of mutual trust and understanding, and a regular, open dialogue between the courts and National Offender Management Service (NOMS) at national level (through the SGC, the Judicial Studies Board (JSB) and in other ways), and at local level, between sentencers and those responsible for commissioning and providing the capacity that is needed.

For the courts to accept such a responsibility would be a new departure, perhaps even a constitutional innovation. But it can surely be argued that since the sentencing provisions of the Criminal Justice Act 2003 create a responsibility for courts to sentence in accordance with the new framework of statutory purposes and SGC guidelines, this should extend to a requirement to have regard to considerations of effectiveness and cost.

To explain that responsibility and persuade, or require, the courts to accept it, is a matter for ministers and the Lord Chief Justice and not for NOMS itself. But to enable courts to discharge that responsibility, NOMS will have to be open and forthcoming in its relations with them, again at national and local levels; to have mechanisms in place which will enable more frequent and more effective communication; and to be responsive in giving effect to the courts' expectations as they gain the understanding and the confidence to express them. 'Contestability'[1] should be applied within those mechanisms and in that spirit. There will need to be a relationship of mutual responsibility and accountability, as well as respect and confidence. Managing that relationship will be a critical function of NOMS's commissioning arm.[2]

Such a development would be as radical for the Prison Service and Probation Service—but more especially the latter—as it would be for the courts. The eventual aim should be a reciprocal process in which prisons and probation offer the court an assessment of an offender's background and situation, the purposes which a sentence might be able to achieve, and an indication of the type of sentence and programme or sentence plan which might enable that to be done. The court should take account of that report in framing its sentence and state the purposes which it hoped would be achieved. NOMS should give effect to the sentence accordingly, and report back to the court on whether the sentence had been successful in those terms or give the reasons if it had not.

---

[1]   The work with offenders conducted under NOMs will be commissioned from agencies in the public sector, private companies and voluntary or charitable organizations. Contestability refers to the philosophy that a more efficient service can be achieved by facilitating competition among the possible service providers.

[2]   NOMS has two arms: one for commissioning services and the other for providing services.

The offender has a central role in the process. Reports on individual offenders would be supplemented by more general reports provided at suitable intervals. Sentencers, court staff, prosecutors, probation and prison staff would meet on a structured and regular basis.

The reference to prosecutors raises an important question about the possible role of the Crown Prosecution Service (CPS) in sentencing. The absence of a role for the prosecutor in sentencing has arguably been an anomaly since the Attorney General's right to refer an unduly lenient sentence—which now extends it to a wider range of offences—to the Court of Appeal was introduced in 1987, but the Criminal Justice Act 2003 provides an even stronger case for courts to hear argument about sentencing, as it does about guilt. That suggestion raises more fundamental questions about the role of the prosecutor in the English system, but it seems to be consistent with the view of Ken MacDonald, Director of Public Prosecutions (DPP) of the future of the CPS (as it is with the hopes that officials had when that service was originally established).

The whole process would be backed by systematic monitoring and research, which would among other things expose any 'sentencing drift'—although correcting that drift of increasingly longer sentences is also of course a more immediate priority.

The approach suggested here is radical, probably more radical than any that those people involved in sentencing reform have so far contemplated. But a radical approach is imperative if the opportunity provided by the 2003 Act and NOMS is not to be wasted, as other opportunities have been wasted in the past.

SOME FURTHER THOUGHTS

The responsible sentence model suggested above deals with the management of people whom the courts have deprived of their liberty by sending them to prison or whose liberty has been restricted by some form of supervision in the community. It is essential to understand the context within which this deprivation of liberty is to be implemented.

When the national prison system was established in England and Wales in the last quarter of the nineteenth century, the context was that of the reform of individuals through a process of personal cleansing, largely within a Christian framework. In the early part of the twentieth century, the context was rehabilitation within a social as well as an individual framework; this was the era of the Borstal institution and the beginning of the probation system.

The context in which restorative justice informs imprisonment is the respect for human dignity and rights. It highlights the fact that those who are in prison or under some other form of court order are more than just offenders. They are first and foremost human beings, with the rights and freedoms shared by all human beings, which can only be restricted in specific circumstances. To use the terms of the famous judgement of Lord Wilberforce in 1982, 'under English law, a convicted prisoner, in spite of his imprisonment, retains all civil rights which are not taken away expressly or by necessary implication' (*Raymond v. Honey*, 1983, A.C. 1). If one accepts this, one must never lose sight of the fact that people who are in prison remain citizens, only restricted by the fact of their deprivation of liberty. Their status as citizens was recently reinforced by a ruling of the European Court of Human Rights that a blanket ban on sentenced prisoners voting in elections violates their human rights.

Using the principles of human decency and rights is also an effective way to manage prisons, one understood by prison practitioners. This context creates the humane and decent environment for which Martin Narey strove throughout all his time as Director General of HM Prison Service from the late 1990s, and which Phil Wheatley, the present Director General, continues to pursue.

The NOMS model as presented is primarily about process, about *how* to do things rather than about what they are meant to achieve. The detail of NOMS is presented in language which is not immediately understood by the uninitiated. The discussion is about how 'individual offenders are to experience their journey through the correctional system'. Each of these journeys is to be 'managed by another person who will own the plan which will determine where the offender's journey will lead'. It is as though the new incarnations of HM Prison Service and the National Probation Service within NOMS exist in a vacuum with no external reference points. In appearing before the court a person becomes transmogrified into 'the offender' and all his or her relations with other people are from now on to be identified solely in terms of the offending. The person is no longer, for example, a father, a brother, a son. He becomes 'the other', someone to be dealt with, someone to be 'managed in a seamless way, end to end', although it is not quite clear what is the final end. This absence of context means that much more will have to be done to develop a reference point to the sort of society we are striving for.

Without a clear understanding of the framework within which NOMS will operate, it is highly probable that the criminal justice agencies will continue to expand, bringing more people into the system who would have been outside their remit in the past. The Carter Report (2003) and the Government's response anticipate that the work of the SGC and the Sentencing Advisory Panel, which will continue to conduct research and generally advise and respond to the SGC, will reduce the risk of this happening. If this is to be the case, there will have to be a stated determination on the part of NOMS not to expand its business.

There are two immediate observations about the NOMS model. The first, as already indicated, is that it deals with people only as offenders. The only identifying feature of the person concerned is that he or she has committed an offence. This is emphasised by the tactic of observing every other feature of his or her humanity through the prism of their offending. This includes family relationships, accommodation needs, employment, social links, health and use of alcohol or drugs. Instead of being features of human existence they become, in the new quasi-professional terminology which has been developed in recent years, 'criminogenic needs'.

The second observation about that model is its emphasis on management. 'Management' is a term usually applied to institutions, situations, organizations or a number of people who come together to form a group, such as a football team. It is not a term which is usually applied to the treatment of individual human beings. The model as presented makes quite clear that the individuals involved are to be regarded, to use Duguid's phrase, as 'objects rather than as subjects' (Duguid, 2000). The closest the proposal comes to recognising the person involved as an active participant is a reference to the need to engage the offender and to secure 'compliance, co-operation and supervision' and 'to work collaboratively with the offender' in order to deliver the sentence plan. Note, collaborative working, not to help the individual to develop as a person with a contribution to make to society — but to deliver the sentence plan.

If we were to try to develop a model which took account of the context in which crime is committed, we would note that most crime is carried out, experienced, reported on and dealt with locally. Those who commit crime and those who are the victims of it frequently live in the same area. For these reasons, it is likely that the solutions to crime and what has become known as 'offending behaviour' will be found locally rather than through any national organization, even one which has regional branches. The involvement of the community to which both offender and victim belong is vital in seeking to resolve the conflict.

If this premise is accepted, it follows that the agencies which carry out the disposals of the court need to be locally based. They need to have close links to the local agencies outside of the criminal justice system which are responsible for accommodation, employment, skills training and support with personal problems, including alcohol abuse and drug abuse. The task of the criminal justice agencies, however they are described, should be to ensure that offenders have access to these local services. Such an approach would be based on the principle of identifying and emphasising the many non-criminal personal features of the individual and helping him or her to strengthen and develop these in a way which will make it less likely that offending will recur. This approach would be in contrast to one which concentrates on identifying negative and potentially criminal features and then attempts to minimise or eliminate them.

PRISONS, RESTORING OFFENDERS AND THE HARMS OF SOCIAL EXCLUSION

Restoration, resettlement, (re)-integration

Three duties and their tasks are fundamental to prisons:

- to treat everyone in their care with respect, decency and humanity;
- to safeguard the physical and emotional safety of staff and prisoners; and
- to prepare prisoners for their eventual release and re-integration back into society.

One of the benefits of the policy of 'end-to-end offender management' is that it may strengthen the Prison Service's commitment to work more effectively to prepare people for resettlement and re-integration. With this in mind, it is important to reconsider the key lessons of the Social Exclusion Unit's (SEU's) Report, *Reducing Re-offending by Ex-Prisoners* (2002) to imagine how prisons can contribute to a reparative and restorative criminal justice experience.

In this section, we discuss the damage that imprisonment causes, and explore the reasons why society should respond to that harm with support. Then, in the final section of this chapter, we discuss nine particular areas of harm and the Government's 'Framework for Reducing Re-offending'.

Prisons and social exclusion

The evidence contained in the SEU Report mentioned above shows some of the negative consequences of imprisonment:

- one-third of prisoners lost their accommodation while in custody;
- two-thirds of prisoners who had jobs, lost them;
- over two-fifths lost contact with their families;
- more than one in five faced increased financial pressures;
- one-third had no accommodation to go to on release; and
- three-quarters said they would not have a job on release.

The harm imprisonment causes is wide-ranging. Retributive values in society support the commitment to inflict harm on wrongdoers. But even so, it would make sense to ensure that, in the long-term, punishment helped to prevent future offending. Instead, many of the effects of prison, such as homelessness, reduced likelihood of employment and fractured family links, have been shown to lead to re-offending.

The purpose of the SEU report was to focus attention on the importance of preparing prisoners for resettlement. The transition from captivity to freedom is a vital time to concentrate on inclusion. Social inclusion is needed in the attitudes of the prisoner and society, to give prisoners a sense of belonging and to encourage each one to think of himself or herself as a citizen with a contribution to make to his or her community and society. Social inclusion is also needed in more practical terms, such as housing, employment, training and rebuilding networks of support which are the keys to achieving a successful resettlement.

Prison can interfere with both processes: the practical work of inclusion is disrupted by the consequences of imprisonment; the change of attitude is often hampered, as society becomes less willing to accept released prisoners back and many prisoners harden in their resentment of society.

So, what can prisons do to offset this damage? In responding to the challenge, where do restorative justice approaches fit in?

Addressing the harm punishment does to offenders and their families

Howard Zehr alludes to the problem that many offenders see themselves as victims. Any reasonable account of the typical background of people in prison (and the SEU report is a good example) bears out the evidence that offenders have experienced extreme disadvantage. The public may sometimes find it difficult to combine the images of offender and victim, to see the whole person who has both offended and been victimised. But consider the facts, set out in the SEU report, as illustrated in *Table 4*.

It is also clear, as the SEU Report convincingly argues, that social exclusion contributes to offending. It would be naïve to suggest that criminality could be traced to any single factor, not least because there are so many different ways of breaking the law. However, there is also no doubt that these factors in combination — drug dependency, unemployment, homelessness, mental distress, and social isolation — are more likely to lead someone to commit further crime than they are to enable them to lead productive and law-abiding lives on their release.

Table 4: Social harms of imprisonment

Disadvantage	Rate in general population	Rate in prison
Suffer two or more mental health problems	5% men 2% women	72% sentenced men 70% sentenced women
Suffer a psychotic disorder	0.5% men 0.6% women	7% sentenced men 14% sentenced women
Unemployed	5%	67%
Reading ability at or below a typical 11 year-old	21-23%	48%
Taken into care as a child	2%	27%
Previous attempt at suicide	[not cited]	20% sentenced men 37% sentenced women
Homelessness	0.9% households	32% prisoners not in permanent accommodation prior to prison

People tend to come to prison already harmed by their social background. A retributive argument is that their experience as victims is no excuse for what they have done. However while this is true — except for the people who are psychotic, prisoners are accountable for their behaviour, as is discussed below — the argument fundamentally misses the point. The point is: unless prior victimisation suffered by prisoners is recognised and addressed, society will be destined to regenerate criminal behaviour and to suffer the effects of re-offending. Unless society acknowledges and repairs the harm done to prisoners and their families by prisons, attempts to reduce re-offending on release are futile.

The aim of restorative justice approaches is for the offender to take responsibility for the harm done. In part this means that the offender needs to own up to the fact that the harm caused by the crime was the result of his or her decisions. But responsibility in restorative terms is primarily forward-looking, as the offender is encouraged to propose a means by which to make amends. Social exclusion is relevant because its impact on offenders has to be acknowledged.

For offenders to play a responsible role in serving their sentence, they need to take whatever opportunities are offered to repair the harm to them caused by previous social exclusion. From the restorative justice perspective, offenders are responsible for addressing the problems they have inherited through their backgrounds of social exclusion because these problems fuel their harmful behaviour towards others. As part of a commitment to make amends, they need to show convincing evidence that they intend not to hurt others in the same way as their present victim.

So what would be the link between an offender's responsibility for the harm caused to his or her victim, and all the harm and pain the offender had previously experienced? In a lecture on victim-offenders, Professor Judith Rumgay raised three points that may begin to answer this question:

- the restorative intervention is primarily focused on the harm that the offender has done to the victim;
- prior harms suffered by the offender are not considered an excuse for the harm that they have caused;
- finding ways to resolve disadvantages they suffered previously might form part of the ways that they take responsibility for the harm they have committed in this particular case.

(Rumgay, 2004)

Why should the state provide prisoners with support?

The theory of restorative justice shows that the state can honour its duties to victims of crime, in part by addressing the needs of prisoners for restoration. Many offenders have experienced, at some time, being a victim of crime or abuse. The effects of social exclusion surface in criminal actions, so that there is a cycle of harm: the person who was victimised victimises others. This is not an excuse for their behaviour, but it is part of the explanation for what occurred. If the goal is to prevent future crime, then all the factors that contribute to offending must be incorporated into the explanation.

Drug addiction cannot justify theft, morally or legally. But when an offence was motivated by the need for drugs, the explanation (and the solutions) must include the person's addiction. The goal of restorative approaches is to solve the problems caused by the offence, and part of this may be to reassure the victim that the offender will not hurt other people in the same way. Part of making amends might require the offender to take steps to address his or her drug problem.

One of the forward-looking implications of restorative justice is the aim to achieve social inclusion for the offender. Social inclusion will require a set of mutual obligations between the offender and society. The offender might come to accept that some of the reasons that he or she harmed others reflected social disadvantages he or she suffered, such as lack of education, unemployment, drug dependency, homelessness or mental illness. Society has an obligation to support the offender in trying to overcome these obstacles.

We are *not* saying that society owes the offender special treatment to make amends for the previous injustice of social exclusion. This would imply that offenders are not responsible for the harm caused by their crimes. What we are advocating is a disciplined and structured problem-solving response to the offender. If the offender understands that a personal transformation is required of him or her so that he or she will not hurt others through criminal activities again, then it makes sense for society to undertake to support that person and not to continue to stigmatise and exclude him or her: working with the offender to prevent the next victim.

The responsibility for making the personal change lies with the offender. Society can facilitate this personal change through, for example, providing offending behaviour courses, drug and alcohol treatment, or education and training. At the opposite extreme, society can choose to continue to ostracise and exclude the offender, despite his or her efforts to go straight. Logically, the end result of this reaction would be that the offender would be far more likely to fail in his or her attempts to change, and far more likely to hurt others by re-offending.

Restorative justice calls for offenders to make a commitment, as a means of taking responsibility for the harm they have caused to others, to address the effects of the abuse or disadvantage. It is this structure—the mutual obligations between prisoners and society, where offenders hold responsibility for personal transformation away from crime and society accepts the duty to support them in that process—which we are proposing as the basis for taking forward the implications of the SEU report.

NATIONAL ACTION PLAN TO REDUCE RE-OFFENDING

The nine challenges for resettlement

The SEU studied, in particular, nine areas of prison and social life, and summarised the damaging impact of prison that can occur:

Education—Can disrupt education in the community.
Employment—Loss of existing employment. Work in prison can reinforce the view of work as mundane and low paid …
Drugs and alcohol – … some prisoners may start to use, others will entrench an addiction …
Mental and physical health—… the experience of imprisonment and subsequent inactivity can exacerbate existing mental illness.
Attitudes and self-control—Other prisoners can reinforce negative attitudes towards crimes and victims.
Institutionalisation and life skills – … can damage prisoners' abilities to think and act for themselves …
Housing—May increase the chance of an offender being homeless. Lack of housing can lead to further problems, such as accessing children in care, health services and benefits.
Benefits and debt—Prison can break the link between offenders and legitimate means of support.
Families—Can lead to financial, emotional and health problems among family members.

(SEU, 2002: 38-39)

These nine areas should be seen as the central challenges for restorative justice's role in resettlement, or in working to achieve inclusion after custody. On the face of it, restorative justice has a lot of potential: its principles of healing, empowerment, inclusion, and personal accountability could help to guide efforts at preparing prisoners for release. But how can prison contribute to the values of offender empowerment, healing and inclusion?

The SEU report put the spotlight on the risk of re-offending. The framework for resettlement, from the SEU perspective, defined these nine areas strictly in terms of their impact on the level of risk of re-offending. In the language of criminology, the SEU offered a deficit-based, rather than strengths-based analysis of the offender's role in the process of resettlement.

In addressing the tasks required to achieve a successful reintegration, the restorative justice priorities are for harms to be repaired and conflicts to be resolved. The nine challenge areas need to be re-defined, so that the key priority in resettlement is to involve the offender in efforts to put things right. Education, training, drug and alcohol treatment, health problems and institutionalisation are areas in which prisoners should be able to access support if they have a genuine desire to desist from crime.

Social inclusion is shorthand for a combination of links that provide a sense of belonging in a family, a neighbourhood, a community, a society and a nation. In practical terms, inclusion means that one can draw on social networks to open up job opportunities. It means significant relationships that provide both emotional support and experience of being held accountable for behaviour. Belonging as a member of a community can include knowing that healthcare needs, educational development and the right to a democratic voice will all be recognised and addressed. It has been argued that most prisoners have never benefited from social integration in the first place.

Restoring offenders through support in these areas, as an exchange of information, expectations and agreements between an offender and a victim, is not the usual sense of restorative justice. But practical support to prevent re-offending can be seen as part of the pieces of the 'solution' to be worked out. The victim might want to see evidence that the person has tried to change, and this might be defined in terms of education or training. For example, training might be a means of gaining skills needed to have sufficient resources to make compensation.

The Action Plan to reduce re-offending in practice
The National Action Plan provides a broad framework, focused on reducing re-offending. It seeks to coordinate all the agencies or services to work together to meet the needs of offenders identified through a case management process and in so doing takes regard of the context of the offending within communities and the services available to those communities. The commentary in this section considers the action plan through a restorative perspective, to inform the application of the work within communities and with concern for the needs of victims of crime as well as offenders.

It is essential that services that impact on offenders at national, regional and local level, work collaboratively in order to help them to reform.

Offenders have also experienced long term disengagement from services, and have histories of poor relationships with those who might help them.
(Paul Goggins, former Minister for Correctional Services and Reducing Re-offending)

Motivating the person who has offended to behave more sociably is the key issue for the criminal justice system. Restorative justice works through three principles:

- *the principle of repair* — justice requires that we work to heal victims, offenders and communities that have been injured by crime;
- *the principle of stakeholder participation* — victims, offenders, and communities should have the opportunity for active involvement in the justice process and as fully as possible; and
- *the principle of transformation in community and government roles and relationships* — the relative roles and responsibilities can be re-thought, and this might be the most challenging aspect of restorative justice. In promoting justice, government is responsible for preserving a just order, and the community for establishing a just peace.

The focus on the needs of the offender looked at through the restorative prison places them in the context of their crimes within communities, families and their victims. It seeks solutions to their needs through working with those stakeholders in meeting their needs as well. Within all the areas of action in the plan, the restorative justice focus provides a wider vision of the person, their life and the reality of the sentence experience for them.

Key action area: framework for reducing re-offending (pp. 6, 7 of Action Plan)

Develop and implement multi-agency regional strategies
Within this work key stakeholders to be identified include local communities, the groups that represent them, victims of crime, and offenders, as well as the range of services that might assist understanding and healing, such as mediation services, self-help groups, health, education, housing and employment services.

Develop an effective case management approach
To be fully restorative, sentence planning would engage not only the offender, but the victim and the community to which the prisoner will one day return. The goals of managing the offender's career should not come top-down from the Home Office. Rather, the plan should develop from the needs of the victim, the support and accountability provided by the community, and the desire in the offender to earn reintegration by making amends.

Sentence planning is also an exercise in personal responsibility by offenders, because their input into the design of the plan is essential. The motivation of the prisoner to be involved in any restorative process will need careful assessment as there has been concern expressed by victims of crime that offenders may be entering the process in order to achieve good reports and therefore earlier release. Thus some distance between sentence planning and gateways to restorative processes are considered good practice.

In ideal circumstances, a prisoner, together with their personal officer, meet early in the sentence to put together a plan that will detail how the time inside will be spent. They draw upon the probation officer's assessment of the offender's needs. Further, they make the plan with a reasonable expectation that resources will be available to meet these needs (whether for drug treatment, anger management, cognitive behaviour programming, or some other intervention).

However, the SEU acknowledged that, at present, almost none of this works as it should. A joint report by the Inspectorates of Probation and Prisons (Home Office, 2001) stated that only about half of prisoners serving between one and four years said that they had a sentence plan; whereas all of them should have had one. Almost half of the sentence plans lacked input from the offender's outside probation officer (SEU, 2002: 40-41).

More important for fulfilling the prison's side of the bargain, the SEU conceded that when sentence plans are made, the programmes that are required to address the offender's problems might not be available. The SEU observed: 'Sentence planning too often is the process of allocating a prisoner to what is available rather than what is needed' (2002: 41) .

The commitment of the offender is central to gaining any credibility within case management. Consultation about the content of the sentence from the start can lead to an acceptance of greater responsibility within the sentence. Involving offenders and their communities of care will be crucial in motivating long term change. There is much evidence that through using restorative meetings the commitment of offenders is increased in addressing the issues within their sentence plan. Restorative meetings prior to release from custody are known to ensure more delivery of agreed plans, with greater satisfaction to all parties.

Establish processes through which agencies can communicate with each other
The focus of this process could be on how best to meet the needs of victims, offenders and their communities whilst maintaining standards of good and safe practice. A key dimension for this sentencing structure is the potential communication with the sentencer so that there is some public accountability for the content of the sentence and its delivery.

Be responsive to the diverse needs of individual offenders
Restorative processes consider the individual needs of those involved and their willingness to work with the process, respecting cultural diversity and raising the awareness of all parties involved.

Working with juvenile offenders
Within the range of community sentences the Youth Justice Board (YJB) has developed expertise in restorative justice practice and processes. This has proved to be very successful in relation to cautioning and in the satisfaction levels of victims, offenders and their families. However the same cannot be said for the custodial experience, where the approach has been mainly to develop

institutions as providing educational opportunities for young people. Any approach involving restorative ideas has often been met by offenders with suspicion, thinking the process is designed to make them feel worse about themselves. When explored further the young people realise that the process of finding out what really happened to all involved and taking some personal responsibility for putting matters right made them feel much better about themselves and led them to become more positive about the opportunities available during their sentence.

Pathway 1: Accommodation (pp. 9-14)

Restorative processes can involve housing authorities in considering the harm caused in the past and developing procedures to avoid any repetition. Any holistic approach to the work arising from a restorative conference will include some reference to accommodation and the sense of community implicit in this matter.

The medium term action involves the development of housing advice. Some of the most impressive pioneering schemes have involved partnerships between staff and prisoners developing information services. There would seem to be much potential to support this work through suitable training and supervision.

One of the chief ways that prisoners can begin to practise taking personal responsibility is to provide services to other prisoners. The accommodation challenge shows that housing advice is a crucial area for prisoners in preparation for resettlement. However, not all prisoners need advice and support to find housing. One prisoner might benefit from training to provide others with housing advice. The St Giles Trust is presently facilitating this training in prisons in the southeast.

Pathway 2: Education, training and employment (pp.15-21)

As the Social Exclusion (SEU) Report showed, the harm done by imprisonment means that the person is likely to be stigmatised by the label of ex-prisoner, and it will be far more difficult for them to find a job.

Education and training are key ways in which the restorative agreement between the offender and the state can be played out. The opportunities prison provides should be negotiated with prisoners through their sentence plan and resettlement focus. This work is having a dramatic impact on the quality of prison regimes where activity is determinedly focussed upon a learning curriculum. Without the motivation of the individual prisoner and a receptive community which supports the changed behaviour, the opportunities of employment and training may leave the prisoner vulnerable to setbacks. The backdrop of developing this context of community is important in sustaining long term change and integration. Restorative conferences in the community as preparation for release can lead to this increased awareness and commitment of members of family and community to build on this important aspect of changed behaviour for many.

Pathway 3: Mental and physical health (pp.23-26)

The emphasis on care and management of support on normal location and the increased possibility of transferring suitable prisoners into community treatment will provide opportunities for further conferences and group discussion. Establishing networks of support in the community is a key component of restorative practice.

A recent study described efforts to engage mental health service users in the assessment and management of their risk. This had benefits in increasing trust, empowering the patient, and improving the accuracy of risk assessments. The authors commented: 'Many service users were aware that they could pose a risk to other people when experiencing psychosis and they wanted help to reduce the chances of this happening' (Langan and Lindow, 2004).

Pathway 4: Drugs and alcohol (pp.27-32)

Many people who go through restorative conferences come to a commitment to treatment through an increased awareness of the destructive effect of their behaviour when influenced by drugs or alcohol. This motivation is vital in bringing about commitment to change and it is important to provide support to keep the person's intent alive.

Pathway 5: Finance, benefit and debt (pp.33-36)

Gaining networks of support and having an awareness of how to use them as well as being willing to admit to the need for help are factors that are often explored through restorative processes. There are issues that involve the need to improve services provided. However, the real change for the person will come from their own awareness of their needs and learning that there are people who have agreed to meet this need, given the changed attitudes.

Pathway 6: Children and families of offenders (pp.36- 40)

Prison Service establishments, including Kirklevington and Blantyre House, have piloted involving families of prisoners in the sentence planning process. While the early indications are positive, a common problem would appear to be that many families do not wish to be involved. The principle of voluntary participation suggests that it would be counter-productive to try to demand that the family attend a conference. But consider the problem from a different perspective.

The question, 'Who has been hurt?' can alert us to the many ways that the crime, and the ways that society has reacted to it, have been harmful to the families of the offenders. Some of the damage is immediately obvious: families can be stigmatised by association; their financial situation is almost inevitably worsened; and relationships are broken, not just by the emotional aftermath of any offence, but by the practical obstacles imprisonment raises in making it difficult to maintain family ties. Children suffer from the temporary loss of a parent—the Prison Reform Trust estimates that over 17,700 children are adversely affected each year as a result of their mothers being imprisoned (PRT, 2003: 2). Other damage to families might be less obvious but is no less real for them, such as their despair when they are faced with disdainful and unsympathetic prison staff.

These reflections might help to explain why some families might be perceived as being reluctant to take part in the processes the prison uses to plan how it will manage the prisoner's sentence. There are also situations in which the victim of the crime and the family of the offender are the same person or people.

As a general rule, the ways offenders' families are harmed by crimes and imprisonment are rarely acknowledged and even less often addressed. If this is true, then a first step in seeking to involve families is to listen to their perspective on what they have lost, what their needs are, and what they would like to happen next.

Any restorative approach seeks to involve family members in discussion about the nature of the harm caused as they have always been affected by the experience of offence, trial and custody. Support for families remains a key aspect that could be improved by NOMS and seeing them as stakeholders in the process of change will transform the way they are considered in sentence planning and delivery. A restorative prism on families would help inform future policies which have been very damaging to relationships in the past.

Prison staff can support families by listening sympathetically to their perspective on how the offence and its aftermath have harmed them, and by taking practical steps to meet the needs of families where the prison has an obligation to do so.

Pathway 7: Attitudes, thinking and behaviour (pp.41-43)

Although this aspect is put last in this document the restorative approach would see it as central to any developmental work during the sentence. The focus in the section is on accredited programmes of cognitive behavioural pedigree and they have a place within the life experience of people who have been disadvantaged through lack of early learning opportunities in life. The emotional intelligence that people gain through restorative approaches can link with the cognitive changes that take place after such courses. The research about discontinuance of offending reveals that a major factor involves a recognition that the person can achieve satisfaction through other means and that the damaging past behaviour, whilst being owned, can be placed into a context of past influences which have now changed. This awareness and the realisation of the damage caused to others are central to the work of restorative justice with offenders. This is always carried out with the assumption that it is the behaviour which is condemned not the person. The person is capable of much more with their potential. This basic optimism can lead to real change in the person's view of themselves—again a major factor in determining whether the criminal behaviour continues.

THE ROLE OF THE PRISON OFFICER

A restorative interpretation of the Action Plan leads to a further implication for the job descriptions of prison officers and managers. Officers will recognise that each prisoner has individual and very complex needs. The impact of prison will affect each prisoner in different ways, and to different degrees. But, more important for this section, the sheer variety of effects that prison might have makes it crystal clear that no single person possesses the expertise required to repair the harm. The central role of the prison officer in the restorative prison is about facilitating, rather than controlling, the process.

This calls for a cultural shift in the officers' understanding of their position in the prison. Back in the 1980s, the Report of the Control Review Committee stated that it was vital that officers maintained control at all times. Security dominated, not only the functions of the prison, but also the skills package prison officers were trained to command.

In the new prison officer role, shaped to fit the requirements of restoration, the officer is a facilitator, whose central task is to bring the prisoner into contact with people from the community whose expertise enables them to respond to the individual needs of each prisoner.

In the restorative prison a typical day might require the officer to:

- arrange a special visit, so that a prisoner nearing release might meet members of the community (including past victims of his or her crimes) into which he or she is being released;
- escort a prisoner to the education area of the prison so that the staff there can link the prisoner to a Further Education College outside which offers a course in his or her chosen field of study;
- contact a neighbourhood dispute centre to invite mediators onto the wing to deal with a dispute between two groups of prisoners;
- schedule a training day, so that prisoners who provide housing advice to other prisoners can gain skills in advice work; and
- sit on a wing conference, convened by a prisoner to resolve a dispute about food portions.

The common thread in these diverse tasks is that the officer's role is essential to make such events happen. The officer is not in control of the events, but is the facilitator who enables these events to occur. The officer links up the prisoner with people from the community who can provide expert support in a wide range of areas. The traditional 'security' role of the officer is always present, but balanced against the more important role of enabling restoration to occur.

PROMOTING SOCIAL RE-INCLUSION

One of the consequences of institutionalisation is that the person who has been in custody for years is likely to have difficulties in handling the levels of personal responsibility expected in everyday life. The SEU Report clearly identifies the ways that people in prison are harmed by the experience. That harm creates obligations, and the communities to which prisoners will return need to undertake the responsibility for supporting reintegration by taking positive steps to undo the damage that prison has done. This makes practical sense, because — as the SEU stresses — when communities address needs like accommodation, rebuilding family ties, and getting ex-offenders into work, the risk of re-offending is dramatically reduced.

The restorative justice perspective on resettlement is that the stigma of the crime, expressed as lingering social exclusion, can only be fully resolved if the offender's obligations to make amends are somehow honoured. (See, for example, Bazemore and Erbe, 2004.) Resolving the persistent conflicts requires government to make available conferences or mediation to all crime victims. The process might result in a pre-release settlement through which the offender agrees never to initiate contact with the victim. It might mean that the offender accepts a duty to continue a programme of drug treatment after they return to the community.

COMMENTS ON THE ACTION PLAN

The Action Plan on Reducing Re-offending has a number of shortcomings:

- it defines the whole person on the basis of their offence — in this it has stigmatising effects;
- it sets out to manage the person's journey through the criminal justice system — in failing to include the person in deciding about the aims and outcomes of a sentence, it is likely to have a disempowering influence; and
- it reduces the human dimensions of the person — for example, their role as a son or daughter — to the risk of re-offending and the concept of 'criminogenic needs'.

A restorative justice perspective provides a healthier balance, with its concern for harm and conflict resolution. Instead of a narrow view that re-offending was all that mattered, the core of resettlement would be enabling the offender to make amends and involving a wide representation of the community to take part in shaping the plan for each person's reintegration. The basic elements of a restorative approach to reintegration are that:

- the harm done to the victim(s) is the first concern;
- all practices in prison show respect for the person;
- prison practices distinguish between harmful behaviour and deficient persons: confronting the actions while respecting the person;
- an inclusive approach to reintegration is used in which decision-making is shared, engaging all who are affected by a crime; and
- time spent in prison is regarded by society, and managed by prisons, as a bridge to full reintegration.

CHAPTER 7

Conclusion

GUIDANCE FOR CRIMINAL JUSTICE AGENCIES

Criminal justice system strategy

Developing restorative practice links the Prison Service to movements within the criminal justice system with the greater focus on meeting the needs of victims of crime, reducing offending and developing approaches to more active citizenship for those involved in the processes – community members, victims of crime, prisoners and the staff who participate.

Prisons can play an important part in the Government's approach to developing restorative justice practice across the criminal justice system, providing opportunities for the most serious offenders and the victims of the most serious crimes to have a restorative meeting.

Prison Service strategy

As well as delivering this most creative aspect of restorative practice the strategic direction of many Prison Service initiatives is supported by restorative practice. There are examples of how this work has helped with safer custody development, with reducing levels of violence in custody, with resettlement and with the general level of motivation of prisoners to become involved in opportunities to address their offending behaviour. With its emphasis on developing relationships within a sense of community there is an implicit assumption about values of personal respect, about treating each other with consideration and decency, with developing a safe environment within which people can take responsibility for their actions, can offer reparation to make good the wrong they have brought about and to be held accountable for their actions.

Resettlement

The delivery of the National Action Plan for Reducing Re-offending is underpinned by restorative practice in the Action areas of Children and Families of Offenders and of Attitudes, Thinking and Behaviour. There is evidence that restorative approaches help the development of motivation in offenders to repair the harm they have caused through their greater awareness of the impact of the damage they have brought about and their empathy towards the victim and others affected by their behaviour. This motivation has helped prisoners to take active responsibility for themselves and others through the completion of agreed commitments to action in repairing the harm done and in avoiding future damaging behaviour.

Active citizenship

The emphasis of restorative justice on developing commitment to repairing the harm caused by crime and the evidence that agreements reached through restorative practice are more likely to be completed than other sanctions or sentence planning processes lead to the development of active citizenship. Prisoners commit themselves to working for the community, the victim and their own supporters through the restorative meeting. Similarly victims often have a different approach towards offenders and the justice process as a result of the restorative meeting, feeling greater satisfaction with the process. Members of the communities of care of the prisoner and the victim understand the complexity of the context of the crime and the impact on the lives of those involved. They often take on a greater commitment to consider the needs of those involved and to work to reduce the harm and prevent further damage.

Victims

Prisons respect the needs of victims when working with the offending behaviour in order to reduce risk. There is a consideration of the need to have done some work involving victim awareness when considering temporary release and there is a commitment to working with the Probation Service to provide information relevant to their victim contact responsibilities. Developing this aspect of the potential role of prisons can be greatly helped by restorative justice concepts.

Many prisoners have been victims of crime themselves. Although this can be difficult to work with in the context of a sentence, where it is expected that the prisoner will take responsibility for their behaviour, it is important for staff to recognise the damage caused by being a victim. Motivation can be greatly limited by the experience.

The inclusion of victim empathy aspects in offending behaviour courses is vital in addressing the serious damage caused and in developing relapse prevention plans. This could be greatly enhanced by further work through restorative processes which focus on meeting the needs of all involved in the crime.

Some prisons are working with the charity Prison Fellowship in delivering the Sycamore Tree Course which involves victims of crime being considered by the participants within an accredited course setting. Prisoners take responsibility for the harm they have caused. This was the subject of a recent evaluation (Research Centre for Community Justice, 2005).

There is an increasing recognition of the experience of communities of care as victims of the crime and a commitment from prisons to work alongside families in establishing a continuing context for returning. Work with families of prisoners is increasingly dealing with the impact of the crime on relationships, attitudes and the capacity for mutual support. Involving family or community of care people in any restorative meeting is crucial in developing a commitment to being together in the future and an awareness of what might help all parties to maintain the intention to remain clear of crime.

Although there is little formal relationship that prisons have with victims of crime, there is experience that when the needs of victims are understood by staff there is a clear commitment to work with the prisoner to reduce risk, and understanding of the purpose of any continuing dialogue and support for any reparative processes that may be agreed through the restorative process.

EXPERIENCE OF RESTORATIVE METHODS IN PRISONS

Restorative Justice in Prisons Project

In 2001 and 2002 a restorative justice project took place in Bristol, Norwich and Winchester prisons. The work involved staff from each prison developing an audit of the areas of conflict in the prison where restorative justice principles could be applied. After some intensive training developmental work began in several areas of prison activity. In Bristol there was an involvement with local groups to develop restorative awareness seminars and drama workshops. This work led to a year's further project with the first restorative justice consultant working in an English prison for a year developing the work. In Norwich there was a commitment to developing local resettlement opportunities for prisoners and the development of a protocol for staff disputes to be dealt with through a process of mediation. In Winchester some work was done in assessing the wish of prisoners on their reception to consider the needs of those affected by their crime, and some consideration to involving families through visits in an understanding of the prison's functions and opportunities.

Prisons where there has been experience of restorative conferencing include:

- Aylesbury;
- Bedford;
- Belmarsh;
- Brixton;
- Bullingdon;
- Feltham;
- Huntercombe;
- Onley;
- Pentonville;
- Reading;
- Spring Hill;
- The Mount;
- Wandsworth;
- Wellingborough;
- Woodhill; and
- Wormwood Scrubs

Potential areas where restorative principles can be applied

Sentence planning

Prisons ask questions about the prisoner's attitude towards the victim of the crime during the sentence planning process. How their concern is handled could lead to a greater awareness of the impact on others and the possibility of some dialogue through the probation service.

Restorative conferencing projects

Many prisons have taken part in the Justice Research Project research programme to consider the effectiveness of restorative conferencing with prisoners on remand and during their sentence. Protocols have been established that enable the work to take place safely for all within the prison context.

Mediation

There is also a long history of mediated meetings between prisoners and their victims through the work of probation projects established in Coventry and Leeds. Mediation between victims and young offenders has been a feature of several establishments, including work done by REMEDI in Sheffield.

Staff awareness of victims' needs

There is much experience of providing training for prison staff at different levels, from training as restorative facilitators to awareness of restorative processes and principles. Victim awareness work has been shown to lead to a better understanding of the context of the crime and the prisoner.

Follow up work by prison staff after a restorative conference is vital if the learning from the event is to be sustained within the experience of the sentence and commitments made are to be honoured by the sentence planning process. By this increased staff awareness, referrals for restorative processes are more likely to be relevant.

Prisoner awareness of restorative justice

Raising the awareness of prisoners to the possibility of restorative processes can lead to many of them thinking about their victims and the impact of the crime on others. As experience of conferencing spreads through prisons there is good evidence that prisoners spread the word about the impact the experience had on them. It has thus become more talked about in those places where several conferences have taken place and the effect has been to make the population more responsive to opportunities. Some prisoners have been trained to be Listeners by the Samaritans, to be available to distressed prisoners who may be considering suicide and wish to speak to a fellow prisoner, and Insiders, experienced prisoners who meet new arrivals to answer questions and help them settle into prison. Along similar lines some prisons in England and Wales are beginning to train and support prisoners in developing mediation skills so that conflict resolution can take place informally through self-referral.

Networking

Sustaining work of a restorative nature needs support from the wider network within the establishment and the service. External organizations, such as the Restorative Justice Consortium and Mediation UK, provide good training, seminars, publications and networks. The Victims Unit at the Home Office provides helpful material to raise awareness. The Restorative Justice Unit in the Home Office is developing the work and is keen to receive feedback about any activity taking place. The Prisoner Administration Group at Prison Service Headquarters is leading on the development of restorative work in prisons.

NEXT STEPS

Restorative approaches have much to offer the Prison Service in seeking to make its operations effective in meeting prisoner and public needs.

The stakes and the possible gains—for victims, for prisoners and for the life of the prison—are high. The risk that efforts will be misunderstood or unappreciated by the public is great. But the traditional prison culture cannot be seen as adequate to the demands of social inclusion, resettlement and reintegration. There is another way to make a difference.

There is a vast potential for using restorative justice to transform the work of prisons. This book has been written at a time of faltering first steps, and is intended to support the efforts of people working in prisons as they refine and nurture restorative practices. The real test will be how much restorative justice can be taken forward in prisons. And those steps depend on you.

Appendix: Two Case Studies

1. Mediation at work in prison

In June 2000 prisoner S, sentenced to five years for fraud, was at Spring Hill prison. He had spent a year in the prison preparing for working out on resettlement, initially on community and then on paid work. He was a trusted prisoner involved with the race relations management group and participating in voluntary activities in the prison.

Having progressed onto resettlement S was working on paid employment in Oxford with a firm of building suppliers. On the particular day in question he returned to the prison and was searched in Reception by G, one of the prison's reception officers, who found that S had a video tucked in at the back of his waistband. As this was the second time to G's knowledge that S had brought in a video and there had recently been an instruction seeking to control such items G placed S on report to the Governor.

The adjudication was taken by the Governor. S admitted he had tried to bring in the video without permission. He complained that G was racist in his approach as he had also searched him the week before, coming out of the kitchen with a bag of foodstuffs and G had insisted they be returned. G had not searched everybody.

The Governor suspended the adjudication and S wrote a formal complaint of racist behaviour. The matter was investigated initially by the Grendon Race Relations Liaison Officer (RRLO) with support from a Spring Hill officer—the two prisons are classified as one establishment. During the investigation the possibility of mediation was discussed with S and G and they both agreed upon it as a way forward. S particularly was anxious to involve the local Community Relations Council (CRC) in the process.

The Aylesbury Community Relations Council has been involved with Spring Hill prison for several years, attending Race Relations Management (RRM) group meetings and assisting with the high numbers of cultural issues raised by the large ethnic minority population—some 25 per cent of the prison's population. With the high level of release on temporary licence Spring Hill uses as a Resettlement prison, there are often sensitivities of equal opportunities concerned with religious and cultural observation issues. The CRC have been very helpful in resolving some of these with the staff.

The mediator who agreed to come into the prison to assist us was a respected member of the community in Aylesbury and knew the prison well. He saw S to hear the complaint. He saw G (accompanied by the RRLO and his Prison Officers Association (POA) friend) and asked for his account of the matter. Then a meeting between G, S, the RRLO and the POA friend was led by a mediator, who outlined events and asked each party for clarification, implications and the way ahead. G apologised to S for his comments—he is renowned for directness in the prison (allegedly a Yorkshire characteristic). S accepted the apology and they shook hands, apparently satisfied.

G got a letter from the Governor after he had received a report of the mediation. The request and complaint process was concluded formally for S and relationships continued in a more understanding way. The adjudication continued with a caution.

G was satisfied with the outcome although he had found it very demanding. He would recommend it to anyone else as a good way of getting to the truth with dignity and being able to continue relationships afterwards. S found it less satisfactory but accepted that the matter had been thoroughly considered and that his complaint had been dealt with seriously. Staff and prisoners regarded the process as important in maintaining relationships of trust. The CRC saw the prison as taking race issues in a serious way and acting on them. The process has been used since to good effect but may not be suitable in every instance, depending on voluntarism, awareness of prison dynamics and trust between mediator and participants.

2. Restorative justice

'Being an inmate, I did some thinking about how to change the way of life I lived, being in and out of prison from the age of 15. I was lucky to be involved with restorative justice in Bullingdon prison and met my victims. It gave me a new way of life and put me on the straight way.

Before I met my victims I did not realise what I had put other people through. You don't think or see the hurt we cause when doing wrong. Meeting my victims was not nice. I was very worried before but willing to change and so went ahead with the meeting. My mum was there and being a good person it was not very nice for her to hear it all. I spoke about everything and did not think it could get any worse. I saw what pain I had caused in doing the things I had done. It gave me bad feelings from seeing things from the victims' point of view. It had me in tears. It changed me and for the good. At the end of the meeting we all shook hands, had tea and a good chat.

Some days after I felt like a new man, ready for the real world again. I thought at the time my mum was going to kill me—just imagine your mum hearing all the bad things you had done. The way she looked at me, I thought she was going to blow up. I felt so ashamed. I can just about imagine myself sitting there, hearing the crime my son had done. It would not be nice especially as it was unexpected.

As a result of the meeting I write a letter each month to keep my victim up to date with what is happening. The experience with my mum has been the most serious thing for me. I have been telling other men in prison about the experience, but only if I think they are serious about wanting to change. Sadly not everyone is, despite the damage they have done.'

[A prisoner, signed and dated]

Glossary of Terms

A selection of terms used in this book, with references, as appropriate, to relevant websites.

ACCT—Assessment, Care in Custody and Teamwork. A new approach to suicide prevention.

Adjudication—In prison, the formal way of responding to a disciplinary charge laid against a prisoner is a hearing run by a governor ('an adjudication'). Typical punishments include a loss of earnings (fines), cellular confinement and loss of evening association (below). If the charge is serious enough to warrant additional days in prison at the end of the sentence and beyond the normal release date then the hearing is conducted by a magistrate.

Association—A daily (usually) time period in prisons when prisoners can freely congregate, play games such as pool or table tennis, use telephones or go to the wing office with a request. The time varies enormously, depending on the type of prison, but association periods usually last about 90 minutes to two hours and are generally held in the evenings, after the meal is finished.

AVP—Alternatives to Violence Project. Courses to develop conflict resolution skills, provided to prisons by volunteer trainers. Website: http://www.avpbritain.org.uk/

Belgian prisons restorative justice—See
http://www.unafei.or.jp/english/pdf/PDF_rms/no61/ch12.pdf

Bullying—Prison bullying defined: one individual establishes a position of domination over another or others. This position is created through a process of intimidation. The position of relative power is exploited. The exploitation persists over a period of time. The Prison Service statement on prison bullying is online at:
http://www.hmprisonservice.gov.uk/adviceandsupport/prison_life/bullying/
For definitions used in schools, see:
http://www.antibullying.net/knowledge/questiononeamore1to5.htm

Central Mediation Services—Work with young offenders at HM Young Offender Institutions (YOIs) Brinsford, Sandwell, West Bromwich. Telephone 0121-525 4659.

Circles of Support and Accountability—Support networks for sex offenders which begin prior to release and continue during the resettlement phase in the community. Web reference:
http://www.restorativejustice.org.uk

Community of care—In a restorative conference, each person directly involved in the crime is invited to bring along some of the people who mean the most to them, and who they feel can support them through the process. This network of support is their community of care.

Complaints—Also known as 'requests and complaints'. HM Prison Service has formal and informal mechanisms for dealing with prisoners' complaints. Prisoners who have a grievance are encouraged, first, to discuss it with an officer, as many problems can be resolved informally. If the problem is not resolved, the prisoner can submit a formal (written) complaint, on a dedicated complaints form. The complaint will be investigated internally, and the prisoner is meant to receive a response within seven days. Prisoners can also make a complaint to the Independent Monitoring Board (IMB)(formerly the Board of Visitors). The ultimate recourse, for prisoners who have gone through these formal steps, is to submit a complaint to the Prisons and Probation Ombudsman. See Prison Service website:
http://www.hmprisonservice.gov.uk/adviceandsupport/prison_life/makingacomplaint
and the Ombudsman's website: http://www.ppo.gov.uk

Criminal justice system—The entire system: police, prosecution, courts, probation and prison services as well as the many other agencies or services that perform other roles.

F2052SH—A form about a prisoner to be completed by staff if there has been any self-harm or if any member of staff is concerned that there may be a risk of self-harm or suicide. The prisoner is registered as at risk, and if the risk is judged to be high, special steps are taken, which can include constant surveillance. The F2052SH is being replaced by ACCT (above).

Induction — The first stage of a prison sentence when a new prisoner is given information about the prison and what is required of him or her in prison. Induction follows reception (below).

IOT—Inside Out Trust: A charity that runs workshops in prisons, providing opportunities to contribute, through repair of bicycles, eyeglasses, or in Braille work, to others less fortunate. A prison workshop of about ten prisoners might repair bicycles which had been donated, so that they can be given to children in developing countries. Website: http://www.inside-out.org.uk

KPI/KPT—Key Performance Indicators and Key Performance Targets are monitoring systems, which record data about regimes and conditions, with the intention of assessing the performance of a prison. For example, the Key Performance Target regarding drug misuse in prison is the percentage of prisoners who test positive on Mandatory Drug Testing (MDT) (below).

Listeners—Volunteer prisoners, trained by the Samaritans, who provide an individual listening service for any prisoner who is feeling depressed or suicidal.

MDT—Mandatory Drug Testing. Each prison is required to test, at random, up to ten per cent of its population each month. These tests provide some indication of the extent of drug misuse in the prison. They can also help staff to identify prisoners who are misusing particular drugs.

Net-widening—A theory that legal structures which were introduced to reduce the prison population can have the opposite effect by bringing more people into the net of criminal justice.

NOMS—National Offender Management Service. The merged services of prisons and probation. NOMS introduced a new national structure, including an Executive Director, Regional Offender Managers (ROMs) who are responsible for commissioning services in each of ten regions, and case management through local offenders managers. The latter will, in theory, oversee the offender's path from pre-sentencing through imprisonment and resettlement, ensuring that an offender receives all the services to which he or she is entitled and that offenders are accountable for fulfilling the requirements of their sentence plans. Website: http://www.homeoffice.gov.uk/inside/org/dob/direct/noms.html

OASYS—Offender Analysis and Assessment System.

PPS—Founded in 1787, Pennsylvania Prison Society advocates on behalf of prisoners and their families and runs voluntary programmes in prisons. Website: http://www.prisonsociety.org/index.shtml

Pre-release — Anything appertaining to preparation for release from prison.

PSO—Prison Service Order, i.e. issued by HM Prison Service HQ affecting the running of prisons, that Governors must follow.

Reception — The location at a prison (usually at or near 'the gate')/or the process whereby prisoners are received into prison.

Safer Custody Group — A part of NOMs headquarters that sets policy on suicide prevention, self-harm and violence reduction in prisons in order to keep those who are in custody safe.

Sentence planning — All prisoners with sentences above four years have a sentence plan that is settled with them by prison and probation staff at the beginning of their sentence.

Sentencing Guidelines Council (SGC) — Independent judicial body established by the Criminal Justice Act 2003 to issue guidelines and associated advice about the sentences they should pass (at their own discretion) to judges and magistrates.

SEU—The Social Exclusion Unit. Set up in 1997 and now within the Cabinet Office. The SEU investigates specific policy areas (such as schools, prisons, and mental health) to make recommendations about how social inclusion can be promoted. Website: http://www.socialexclusion.gov.uk

Sycamore Tree Project—A faith-based project working with prisoners on the impact of their behaviour on victims. Web reference: http://www.restorativejustice.org.uk/About_restorative justice/pdf/SycamoreTree.pdf

VOM—Victim-Offender Mediation, a special form of mediation developed to enable victims and offenders to communicate in the aftermath of a crime, either directly or indirectly (by the mediator speaking separately to both parties).

VRS—Violence Reduction Strategy: an approach pioneered by HM Prison Service Safer Custody Group, defined in Prison Service Order 2750. Website: http://pso.hmprisonservice.gov.uk/PSO_2750_violence_reduction.doc

References

Barton, Charles (2000) 'Empowerment and Retribution in Criminal Justice,' in Strang and Braithwaite, 55-76.

Bazemore, Gordon and Carsten Erbe (2004) 'Reintegration and Restorative Justice: Towards a Theory and Practice of Informal Social Control and Support', in Maruna and Immarigeon.

Boyack, Jim, Helen Bowen and Chris Marshall (2004) 'How Does Restorative Justice Ensure Good Practice?' in Zehr and Toews, 265-271.

Boyes-Wilson, Carolyn (2004) 'What Are the Implications of the Growing State Involvement in Restorative Justice?' in Zehr and Toews, 215-226.

Braithwaite, John (1993) *Juvenile Offending: New Theory and Practice*, Australian Institute of Criminology, online: http://www.aic.gov.au/publications/proceedings/22/braithwa.pdf

Braithwaite, John and Heather Strang (2000) 'Connecting Philosophy and Practice', in Strang and Braithwaite, eds.

Burton, John (1990) *Conflict: Resolution and Prevention*, London: The Macmillan Press Ltd.

Carter, Patrick (2003) 'Managing Offenders, Reducing Crime: A New Approach,' http://www.homeoffice.gov.uk/docs2/managingoffenders.pdf

Cavanagh, T. (1998) 'Adopting New Values for the Courts: What is Restorative Justice?' *The Court Manager*, 13(2/3) 24-27. Williamsburg, VA: National Association for Court Management.

Christie, Nils (1977) 'Conflicts as Property,' *British Journal of Criminology* 17: 1-26.

Cooke, David J (1992) 'Prison Violence and Inmate Suicide and Self-Injury', online: http://www.csc-scc.gc.ca/text/pblct/forum/e043/043k_e.pdf

Daly, Kathleen (2000) 'Revisiting the Relationship between Retributive and Restorative Justice', in Strang and Braithwaite, 33-54.

Department of Justice, Canada (2001) 'The Effectiveness of Restorative Justice Practices: A Meta-Analysis', by Jeff Latimer, Craig Dowden and Danielle Muise, Canada: Research and Statistics Division.

Duguid, Stephen (2000) *Can Prisons Work? The Prisoner as Object and Subject in Modern Corrections*, Toronto, Canada: University of Toronto Press.

Edgar, Kimmett and Carol Martin (2004) 'Perceptions of Race and Conflict: Perspectives of minority Ethnic Prisoners and of Prison Officers', Home Office Online Report 11/04: http://www.homeoffice.gov.uk/rds/pdfs2/rdsolr1104.pdf

Edgar, Kimmett, Ian O'Donnell and Carol Martin (2003) *Prison Violence: The Dynamics of Conflict, Fear and Power*, Devon: Willan Publishing.

Goffman, Irving (1961) *Asylums*, New Jersey: Anchor Books.

HM Chief Inspector of Prisons (1999) *Suicide is Everybody's Concern*, A Thematic Report, London: HM Prisons Inspectorate.

Home Office (2001) *Through the Prison Gate: A Joint Thematic Review by HM Inspectorates of Prisons and Probation*, London: HMSO.

Hoyle, Carolyn, Richard Young and Roderick Hill (2002) *Proceed with Caution: An Evaluation of the Thames Valley Police Initiative in Restorative Cautioning*, York: Joseph Rowntree Foundation.

Immarigeon, Russ (2004) 'What is the Place of Punishment and Imprisonment in Restorative Justice?' in Zehr and Toews (2004), 143-154.

JCHR: Parliamentary Joint Committee on Human Rights (2004) *Deaths in Custody, Third Report of Session 2004-5*, Vol 1., London: House of Lords; House of Commons.

Johnson, Gerry and Kevan Scoles (1999), *Exploring Corporate Strategy*, fifth edition, New Jersey: Prentice Hall.

Johnstone, Gerry (2002) *Restorative Justice: Ideas, Values, Debates*, Devon: Willan Publishing.

Langan, Joan and Lindow, Vivien (2004) 'Mental Health Service Users and their Involvement in Risk Assessment and Management', Joseph Rowntree Foundation, online: www.jrf.org.uk/knowledge/findings/socialcare/414.asp

The Leuven Declaration (1997) *The Leuven Declaration on the Advisability of Promoting the Restorative Approach to Juvenile Crime*, Leuven, Belgium: First International Conference on Restorative Justice for Juveniles – Potentialities, Risks and Problems for Research.

Liebling, Alison (2004) *Prisons and their Moral Performance: A Study of Values, Quality and Prison Life*, with Helen Arnold, Oxford: Clarendon Studies in Criminology, Oxford University Press.

Liebmann, Marian and Stephanie Braithwaite, (1999) *Restorative Justice in Custodial Settings*, Northern Ireland: The Restorative Justice Working Group in Northern Ireland; online: http://www.restorativejustice.org.uk/simple/About_restorative justice/pdf/Restorative%20justice%20in%20custodial%20settings_Marian%20Liebmann%20and% 20Stephanie%20Braithwaite.pdf

McCold, Paul (2004) 'What Is the Role of Community in Restorative Justice Theory and Practice?' in Zehr and Toews (2004), 155-172.

McCold, Paul and Ted Wachtel (2002) 'Restorative Justice Theory Validation,' in E. G. M. Weitekamp and H. J. Kerner, eds. (2002) *Restorative Justice: Theoretical Foundations*, Devon: Willan Publishing, 110-142.

Marshall, Tony (1999) *Restorative Justice: An Overview*, London: The Home Office.

Maruna, Shadd and Russ Immarigeon, eds. (2004) *After Crime and Punishment: Pathways to Offender Reintegration*, Devon: Willan Publishing.

Miers, David, Mike Maguire, Shelagh Goldie, Karen Sharpe, Chris Hale, Ann Netten, Steve Uglow, Katherine Doolin, Angela Hallam, Jill Enterkin and Tim Newburn (2001) *An Exploratory Evaluation of Restorative Justice Schemes*, Crime Reduction Research Series Paper 9, London: Home Office Research Development and Statistics Directorate.

Mika, Harry and Howard Zehr (2002) 'Signposts', *Conciliation Quarterly* Vol. 20, No. 3; online: http://www.restorativejustice.org/rj3/Feature/2002/MARCH2002/Conciliation/signposts.htm.

Minow, Martha (1990) *Making all the Difference: Inclusion, Exclusion and American Law*, New York: Cornell University Press.

Morris, Allison and Warren Young (2000) 'Reforming Criminal Justice: The Potential of Restorative Justice', in Strang and Braithwaite, 11-31.

Morrison, Brenda (2002) 'Bullying and Victimisation in Schools: A Restorative Justice Approach', Canberra: Australian Institute of Criminology; online: http://www.aic.gov.au

New Zealand Ministry of Justice (1995) *Restorative Justice: A Discussion Paper*, Wellington: Ministry of Justice.

O'Donnell, Ian and Kimmett Edgar (1996) 'Victimisation in Prisons', Home Office Research Findings No. 37, London: The Home Office.

Pelikan, Christa (2000) *Victim-Offender Mediation in Domestic Violence Cases: A Research Report*, Vienna: UN Crime Congress Ancillary Meeting.

Prison Reform Trust (2003) *Having Their Say: The Work of Prisoner Councils*, by Enver Solomon and Kimmett Edgar, London: Prison Reform Trust.

Quill, D and J Wynne (1990) *Victim Offender Mediation Handbook*, London: Save the Children (available from Mediation, UK).

Research Centre for Community Justice (2005) 'Evaluation of the Sycamore Tree Programme', by Simon Feasey, Patrick Williams and Rebecca Clarke, available from Prison Fellowship: enquiries@prisonfellowship.org.uk or Online: www.prisonfellowship.org.uk

Restorative Justice Consortium (2004) *Principles of Restorative Processes, 2004*; London: Restorative Justice Consortium; online: http://www.restorativejustice.org.uk/simple/?Resources:Best_Practice:Principles

Restorative Justice Consortium, 'About Restorative Justice' Online: http://www.restorativejustice.org.uk/about-rj/index.htm.

Restorative Justice Online (1997) Christopher Bright, ed., 'What is Restorative Justice,' Online: http://www.restorativejustice.org/rj3/intro_default.htm.

Robert, L and T Peters (2003) 'How Restorative Justice is Able to Transcend the Prison Walls: A Discussion of the "Restorative Detention" Project', in: EGM Weitekamp and H-J Kerner (eds.) *Restorative Justice in Context: International Practice and Directions*, Devon: Willan Publishing.

Social Exclusion Unit (2002) *Reducing Re-Offending by Ex-Prisoners*, London: The Social Exclusion Unit.

Sparks, Richard, Tony Bottoms and Will Hay (1996) *Prisons and the Problem of Order*, Oxford: Clarendon Studies in Criminology, Oxford University Press.

Strang, Heather and John Braithwaite, eds. (2000) *Restorative Justice: Philosophy to Practice*, Aldershot: Ashgate.

Thames Valley Partnership (2002) *Restorative Justice in Prisons*, Tim Newell, Thames Valley Partnership.

Toch, Hans (1992) *Living in Prison: The Ecology of Survival*, Washington, DC: American Psychological Association.

Toews, Barbara (2002) 'Listening to Prisoners', *VOMA Journal*, Russ Immarigeon, ed., International Victim Offender Mediation Association, Summer 2002 Issue Number 11.

Toews, Barbara and Jackie Katounis (2004) 'Have Offender Needs and Perspectives been Adequately Incorporated into Restorative Justice?' in Zehr and Toews, 2004.

United Nations Commission on Crime Prevention and Criminal Justice's Meeting of Experts in Ottawa, Canada (2002) 'Basic Principles on the Use of Restorative Justice Programmes in Criminal Matters,' Economic and Social Council E/CN.15/2002/L.2/Rev.1.

van Ness, Dan (1998) 'Restorative Justice: International Trends', Wellington, New Zealand: Victoria University. Online: http://www.restorativejustice.org/resources/docs/vanness13/download

van Ness (2004), Online: http://www.restorativejustice.org/rj3/restorative justice_City/Documents/Van_Ness_paper_1.htm 24 November, 2004.

Walgrave, Lode (2004) 'Has Restorative Justice Appropriately Responded to Retribution Theory and Impulses?' in Zehr and Toews (2004), 47-60.

Wright, Martin (1999) *Restoring Respect for Justice*, Winchester: Waterside Press.

Zehr, Howard (1990/1995) *Changing Lenses: A New Focus for Crime and Justice*, Pennsylvania: Herald Press.

Zehr, Howard (2002) *The Little Book of Restorative Justice*, Pennsylvania: Good Books.

Zehr, Howard and Barbara Toews (eds) (2004) *Critical Issues in Restorative Justice*, Devon: Willan Publishing.

Index

Diagrams, Figures, Tables and Boxes

A selection of books from **Waterside Press**
with a Restorative essence that can be found at

www.watersidepress.co.uk

or telephone (+44)(0)1962 855567

Justice for Victims and Offenders
A Restorative Response to Crime
Martin Wright

Restoring Respect for Justice A Symposium
Martin Wright

Conflict Resolution A Foundation Guide
Susan Stewart

Relational Justice Repairing the Breach
Edited by Jonathan Burnside and Nicola Baker
With a Foreword by Lord Woolf
In association with the Relationships Foundation, Cambridge, UK.
Contributors include:
**Anthony Bottoms, Andrew Coyle, David Faulkner, John Harding,
Judge (Fred McElrea) and Michael Schluter**

Criminal Punishment and Restorative Justice
Past, Present and Future Perspectives
David J Cornwell
With a Foreword by Tony Cameron
Contributions by:
Judge (Fred) McElrea, John R Blad and Robert B Cormier
For further details see the panel overleaf